John Robert Lunn

Of Motion; An Elementary Treatise

Anatiposi

John Robert Lunn

Of Motion; An Elementary Treatise

Réimpression inchangée de l'édition originale de 1859.

1ère édition 2023 | ISBN: 978-3-38274-430-4

Anatiposi Verlag est une marque de Outlook Verlagsgesellschaft mbH.

Verlag (Éditeur): Outlook Verlag GmbH, Zeilweg 44, 60439 Frankfurt, Deutschland
Vertretungsberechtigt (Représentant autorisé): E. Roepke, Zeilweg 44, 60439 Frankfurt, Deutschland
Druck (Imprimerie): Books on Demand GmbH, In de Tarpen 42, 22848 Norderstedt, Deutschland

OF MOTION.

AN ELEMENTARY TREATISE

JOHN ROBERT LUNN, M.A.

FELLOW AND LADY SADLEIR'S LECTURER OF S. JOHN'S COLLEGE.

CAMBRIDGE:
DEIGHTON, BELL, AND CO.
LONDON: BELL AND DALDY.
1859.

PREFACE.

MY object in the following pages has been to put forth the principles of the Science of Motion in their true geometrical form, postponing the consideration of force (the properties of which are presumed to have been fully investigated in Statics) until the reader may be able to separate in his mind the geometrical ideas from the mechanical. To the fact that these ideas are not kept separate at the outset I apprehend that the want of clearness in the student's mind about the real investigation that does take place in any case may be attributed.

Until a comparatively recent period all works on this subject have been concerned with answering the question, Given the *force* acting on any body, how will it move? But how a *motion* is to be estimated, which of course is a preliminary question that should be fully investigated, on this point very little has been said. The first book, I think, in which the geometry of Motion was formally treated of, separate from the cause, was Griffin's *Dynamics of a Rigid Body;* this of course could not be referred to till the elements of the subject had been mastered. The same method of treatment was adopted in Sandeman's excellent treatise *Of the Motion of a Single Particle;* a work to which I am greatly indebted, as the reader will easily see, the 6th chapter being very little else than a transcript of his second chapter on the Laws of Motion. There is one defect in that work, but for which the present treatise would never have appeared: it is, that a certain amount of previous knowledge of the subject is almost necessary, and the work itself is inadmissible in the case of those who are unacquainted with the Differential Calculus. This introductory position I propose to take up.

I have written this book so that a knowledge of the Differential Calculus is not necessary; the student, by simply omitting the articles marked Δ, will become acquainted with the Science of Motion as far as he can by the application of the lower analysis only: such an one I presume to proceed to the first three sections of Newton's *Principia*, which will take the place of my 4th chapter; and I may remark in passing, that in them Newton always uses the word "force" as *synonymous* with "acceleration;" and I think that if any editor of Newton should in future replace the words "force" and "body" by "acceleration" and "point," he will do good service to the cause of philosophy.

But I have also considered the case of those, who, knowing the Differential Calculus, still confine themselves to the elementary portions of the Science of Motion: to such readers it is scarcely sufficient merely to indicate the method to be pursued, as is done in Sandeman's first chapter, but actually to deal with the most ordinary cases of Motion in a geometrical manner before applying ourselves to cases of nature.

Those who purpose to follow the subject throughout, may perhaps find this treatise useful, and for the higher portions of it may be referred to Sandeman's work.

For the benefit of these last two classes of readers the articles marked Δ are intended.

In the first four chapters I have confined myself entirely to the *phœnomena* of Motion, that is, I have treated of what has hitherto been called (though not universally) Kinematics: this name would have been given to the present treatise, had it not been that it was thought open to objection; other names were suggested, which were in their turn objected to* : I did not therefore adopt any one, not being desirous of controversy: it is to be hoped that scholars will soon agree upon a name that will be satisfactory.

I may be thought a purist in my nomenclature, but it seems at least a fault on the right side, especially in a work on first principles: for the furtherance of my purpose of keeping the reader's mind free from any idea of force in his considering motion abstractedly, I have rejected the usual symbol f for an acceleration, using instead a; for the actual choice of f would in my opinion naturally lead the reader to think of force. For a similar reason, in Chapter IV. I have adopted λ instead of μ: this latter having been hitherto said to represent the "absolute *force*."

In subsequent chapters this treatise becomes Dynamical: and in them I have endeavoured to shew how in any case we get rid of force, and investigate the motion geometrically; most of the cases of motion considered are brought under the formulæ in the first four chapters. I have rather avoided representing the intensity of a force by the product of the mass moved and the acceleration produced, as the beginner would not be very likely to have a clear notion of this: this is more especially true of those Articles in which the Differential Calculus is not employed: in the other Articles I have not so rigidly restricted myself.

---

* J. Hermann (1716) and Kant use the word *Phoronomy*.

An Appendix is added, containing certain geometrical properties of the cycloid, which it was necessary to assume; and a number of problems, selected principally from recent Examination Papers in the Senate-House and S. John's College.

I have to thank those friends who have in many ways assisted me in this work, especially Professor Sandeman, M.A. of Queens' College, who permitted me to make unlimited use of his valuable treatise mentioned above, Mr W. H. Besant, M.A. of S. John's College, Rev. N. M. Ferrers, M.A. of Caius College, and Mr E. Wilson, M.A. of Trinity College.

CONTENTS.

CHAPTER I.

GENERAL PRINCIPLES.—OF VELOCITY AND ACCELERATION.

CHAPTER II.

Of the Motion of a Point in general. Analytical Expressions for Velocities and Accelerations in certain directions.

CHAPTER III.

Of the Motion of a Point affected by a constant Acceleration, the direction of which is always the same.

CHAPTER IV.

Of the Motion of a Point affected by an Acceleration, the direction of which always passes through a Fixed Point.

CHAPTER V.

OF MATTER AND FORCE.

CHAPTER VI.

OF THE DYNAMICAL LAWS OF FORCE, COMMONLY CALLED THE LAWS OF MOTION.

CHAPTER VII.

OF CERTAIN CASES OF FREE MOTION IN NATURE.

CHAPTER VIII.

OF CONSTRAINED MOTION OF PARTICLES.

CHAPTER IX.

OF IMPULSES AND COLLISION OF PARTICLES.

APPENDIX.

OF THE CYCLOID.

OF MOTION.

CHAPTER I.

1. IF a point change its position in space it is said to move.

2. All motion has reference to space and time, and since a point may, under different circumstances, pass over different spaces in equal intervals of time, or require different intervals of time to pass over equal spaces, the mind necessarily conceives the idea of quickness or slowness of motion. The degree of this quickness or slowness is called velocity.

3. If the moving point pass over equal spaces in equal successive intervals of time, its velocity is said to be uniform. It is evident that the velocity of a moving point will be greater or less in exact proportion as the space it passes over in any given time is greater or less, or as the time required for the point to pass over any given space is less or greater; so that the measure of the velocity varies as the space passed over when the time is constant, and inversely as the time when the space is constant, i.e. if v be the measure of the velocity with which a moving point describes a space s in a time t, $v \propto \dfrac{s}{t}$.

L.   B

4.   If, with the unit of velocity, a space σ be described in time τ, we shall have

$$v : 1 :: \frac{s}{t} : \frac{\sigma}{\tau};$$

$$\therefore v = \frac{\tau}{\sigma} \cdot \frac{s}{t}.$$

As σ and τ are perfectly arbitrary, we may assume any values we please for them.   The simplest assumption is that

$$\tau = 1, \ \sigma = 1, \text{ and then } v = \frac{s}{t}.$$

If $t = 1$, $v = s$.

5.   The assumptions we have made determine the unit of velocity to be that with which the unit of space is described in the unit of time; and the measure of any velocity to be the space passed over in an unit of time.

The units of space and time are perfectly arbitrary.

6.   Since the simplicity of an investigation depends greatly upon the choice of units, it may often be advantageous to obtain an expression for a velocity in terms of other units of space and time than those in terms of which it is already expressed.

Thus, suppose we wish to obtain the measure of a velocity in terms of a new set of units of space and time, a and b times respectively as great as the original units.   If v be the measure of the velocity referred to the original units, the moving point would describe the space v in the unit of time, and therefore it would describe the space bv in the new unit of time, which is b times as great as the former; therefore, as the new unit of space is a times as great as the former, the number of such units described will be $\frac{bv}{a}$; this, therefore, is the measure of the velocity sought.

E. g.   If the velocity of a moving point be measured by 20 when a foot and a second are the units of space and time, what will be its measure when a yard and a minute are the units?

The point would move over 20 feet in $1''$,

and therefore over 20×60 feet in $60''$ or $1'$,

and therefore over $\dfrac{20 \times 60}{3}$ yards in $1'$;

therefore the measure of the velocity is 400.

In common language, the rate of 20 feet per second is the same as that of 400 yards per minute.

7. If s be the space passed over in time t by a point moving uniformly with a velocity v, then will $s = vt$. For v units of space are passed over in the unit of time, and therefore vt units of space are passed over in the time t, i.e. $s = vt$.

If a be the initial distance of the moving point from a fixed point in its path, and s the distance at time t, then $s = a + vt$, provided that the point be moving *away from* the fixed point. If however it be moving *towards* it, s will $= a - vt$.

This shews that if we write $-v$ for v, we reverse the direction of the motion; or, in other words, if velocities in any one direction be considered positive, those in the opposite direction must be considered negative.

We may obviously represent a velocity by a straight line drawn in the direction of the motion, and equal in length to the magnitude of the measure of the velocity, so that if a point were to move uniformly along the line, it would arrive at the extremity of it at the end of an unit of time.

8. The Parallelogram of Velocities.

" If two adjacent sides of a parallelogram represent in magnitude and direction two velocities simultaneously existing in the motion of a point, the resulting velocity will be represented in magnitude and direction by the diagonal drawn through the point of intersection of those two sides."

In order to conceive the motion more clearly, let the point be supposed to be compelled to move uniformly along the line AB, while AB is transferred so as to be always parallel to itself, its extremity moving uniformly along AC.

Let AB, AC represent the coexisting velocities. At the end of an unit of time the point will have moved over the space AB, but the line AB has then arrived at the position CD, therefore the point will be found at D, the opposite angle of the parallelogram BC.

Let ab be the position of the line AB, and d the position of the moving point in it, at any other instant of the motion. Join AD, Ad.

Then $ad : CD ::$ time required for the point to move over ad

: time required for it to move over CD

(because the motion is uniform),

i.e. as the time in which the extremity of the line ab moves over Aa : the time in which it moves over AC,

i.e. as $Aa : AC;$

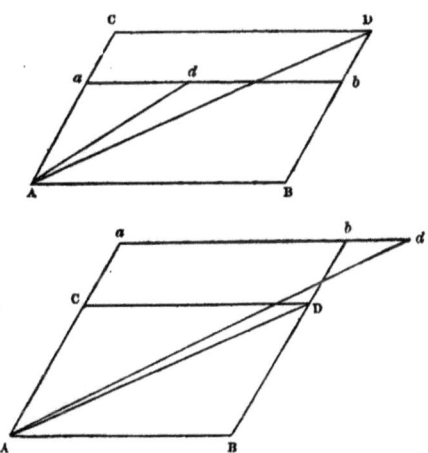

therefore the triangles Aad, ACD have equal angles at a, C, and the sides containing them proportional; therefore they are equiangular, i.e. the angles aAd, CAD are equal;

therefore d is in the diagonal AD, and consequently the moving point passes along AD.

Also it describes AD uniformly,

for $Ad : AD :: Aa : AC$

:: time in which the extremity of ab passes over Aa

: time in which it passes over AC

:: time in which the moving point passes in space over Ad

: time in which it passes over AD;

$\therefore AD$ represents the resulting velocity in magnitude and direction (Art. 7).

9. This may be extended to space of three dimensions, as follows:

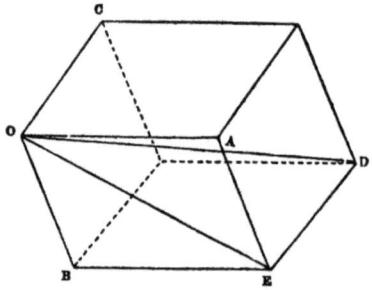

If OA, OB, OC represent in magnitude and direction three coexistent velocities, OD the diagonal of the parallelepiped constructed on OA, OB, OC as edges, will represent the resulting velocity both in magnitude and direction.

For the velocities OA and OB are equivalent to a velocity OE, and therefore OA, OB, OC are equivalent to OE and OC, and consequently to OD.

This proposition is called the parallelepiped of velocities.

10. From this it is clear that we may consider any given velocity to result from the coexistence of other velocities in two or three given directions, according as we deal with space of two or three dimensions, and this is called resolving a velocity.

It is usual to resolve into directions at right angles with each other, and in that case if OC represent the velocity v, and the angle $COx = \theta$,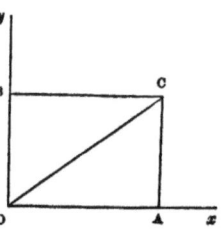
the velocity in Ox will be represented by OA, i.e. $OC \cos \theta$, and therefore $= v \cos \theta$;
and the velocity in Oy will be represented by OB, and therefore $= v \sin \theta$.

If we deal with space of three dimensions, OD representing the velocity v, and the angles DOx, DOy, DOz, being called α, β, γ,

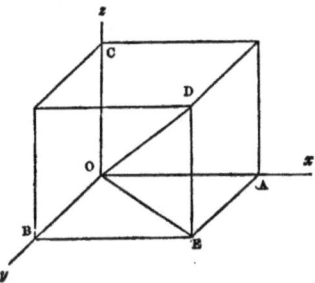

$$
\begin{aligned}
\text{the velocity in } Ox \; &= OA = v \cos \alpha \\
\cdots\cdots\cdots\cdots \; Oy \; &= OB = v \cos \beta \\
\cdots\cdots\cdots\cdots \; Oz \; &= OC = v \cos \gamma
\end{aligned} \Bigg\}.
$$

These are called the resolved parts of the velocity v.

11. Conversely, having given the velocities in given directions in space, we can find an analytical expression for the resulting velocity in magnitude and direction. This is called compounding the given velocities.

For if in space of two dimensions, the velocities along Ox and Oy be given $= v_1, v_2$, respectively, we have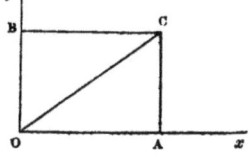

$$OC^2 = OA^2 + OB^2,$$

$$\tan COx = \frac{OB}{OA},$$

i.e. $v^2 = v_1^2 + v_2^2$; $\tan \theta = \dfrac{v_2}{v_1}$.

Or otherwise, $v_1 = v \cos \theta$, $v_2 = v \sin \theta$; whence the same results are obtained.

If we consider space of three dimensions, and the velocities along Ox, Oy, Oz be given $= v_1$, v_2, v_3,

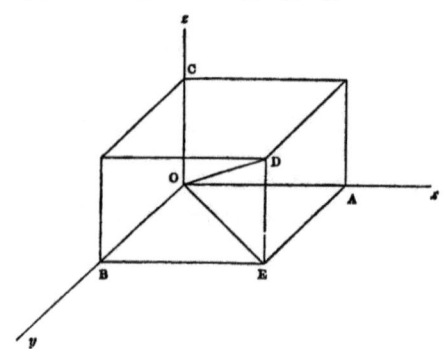

we have
$$OD^2 = OE^2 + ED^2,$$
$$= OA^2 + OB^2 + OC^2,$$
$$\cos DOx = \frac{OA}{OD}, \quad \cos DOy = \frac{OB}{OD}, \quad \cos DOz = \frac{OC}{OD};$$
i.e. $\quad v^2 = v_1^2 + v_2^2 + v_3^2,$
$$\cos \alpha = \frac{v_1}{v}, \quad \cos \beta = \frac{v_2}{v}, \quad \cos \gamma = \frac{v_3}{v}.$$

Or otherwise, $v \cos \alpha = v_1$, $v \cos \beta = v_2$, $v \cos \gamma = v_3$, whence, as by a well-known theorem, $\cos^2 \alpha + \cos^2 \beta + \cos^2 \gamma = 1$, the same results are obtained.

12. If v be the velocity of a point in the direction of a line whose direction-cosines are l, m, n, the resolved part of this in the direction of another line whose direction-cosines are l', m', n', will equal

$v \times$ cosine of the angle between the lines
$= v (ll' + mm' + nn')$
$= lv . l' + mv . m' + nv . n';$

lv, mv, nv, are the resolved parts of the given velocity in the directions of the co-ordinate axes, and as l', m', n', are the cosines of the angles between these and the second line, this proposition shews that the resolved part required may be correctly obtained by resolving the given velocity into three directions at right angles to each other, and taking the sum of these resolved separately upon the second line.

13. We have hitherto considered velocity as uniform: but it is plain that the velocity of a moving point may be continually changing, and we must fix a measure for such a velocity.

If another point be moving uniformly with that velocity with which the proposed point is moving at the instant under consideration, this velocity is measured by the space which the point passes over in an unit of time, and consequently we must measure the varying velocity by the space which *would* be passed over in an unit of time, supposing that the velocity were to remain constant for that unit of time.

14. We shall now obtain a relation between the space, time, and velocity in such a case.

If s be the space passed over in time t reckoned from the instant under consideration, and if s' be the space which *would* be described in time t supposing the velocity constant, we have as before (Art. 4),

$$v = \frac{s'}{t},$$

and this is true always, whatever be the magnitudes of s' and t; therefore it is true when s' and t are indefinitely diminished, in which case

$$v = \text{Limit} \frac{s'}{t} = \text{Limit} \frac{s}{t};$$

because s and s' are ultimately equal.

Δ. 15. If we employ the differential calculus, we shall obtain the same result. For if a space δs be described in a small time δt immediately subsequent to the instant under consideration, and if v', v'' be the greatest and least values of the velocity during the time δt, it is plain that $\delta s < v' \delta t$, and $> v'' \delta t$;

$$\therefore \ \frac{\delta s}{\delta t} < v', \text{ and } > v'',$$

and making δs, δt indefinitely small, as v', v'' have both the same limit v, we get

$$\frac{ds}{dt} = v.$$

16. This result includes the case of a constant velocity, because in that case $\frac{s}{t}$ being constant is not altered by taking s and t indefinitely small,

$$\text{or } \frac{s}{t} = \text{Limit} \frac{s}{t}, \text{ or} = \frac{ds}{dt}.$$

17. The propositions called the parallelogram and parallelepiped of velocities are equally true for varying velocities, as may be clearly seen by considering an indefinitely small parallelogram or parallelepiped similar to those in the figures of Arts. 8, 9, or by comparing the motion of the proposed point with that of another moving with - constant velocities equal to those in question.

18. If the velocity of a moving point be continually increased, its motion is said to be accelerated; and if diminished, retarded.

The terms acceleration and retardation* are used to express the *degree* of this change of velocity.

The acceleration or retardation is uniform when the velocity is uniformly increased or diminished, i. e. when equal velocities are acquired in equal successive intervals of time, in or opposite to the direction in which the motion is estimated.

19. An uniform acceleration is clearly greater or less in exact proportion as the velocity acquired by the moving point in a given time is greater or less, or as the time requisite for the moving point to acquire a given velocity is less or greater.

Therefore if α be the measure of an acceleration, owing to which the moving point acquires a velocity v in time t, $\alpha \propto \frac{v}{t}$,

---

* N.B. We are here concerned with acceleration and retardation merely as matters of fact, and not considered as resulting from any particular cause whatever.

L.

C

and if with the unit of acceleration a velocity v_1 is acquired in time t_1, we have

$$a : 1 :: \frac{v}{t} : \frac{v_1}{t_1},$$

and therefore

$$a = \frac{t_1}{v_1} \cdot \frac{v}{t};$$

t_1 and v_1 are at present arbitrary, and the simplest assumption we can make respecting them is that they both $= 1$, and then $a = \frac{v}{t}$. If $t = 1$, $a = v$.

20. These assumptions fix the unit of acceleration to be that owing to which the unit of velocity is acquired by the moving point in the unit of time, and the measure of any acceleration to be the velocity which is acquired in the unit of time.

An acceleration then may be represented by a line, both in magnitude and direction.

The same remarks apply to retardations.

21. Hence if v be the velocity acquired in time t by means of an uniform acceleration a, v will $= at$, because a velocity a is acquired in each unit of time.

And if v', v be the velocities at the beginning and end of the time t,

$$v = v' + at \text{ if the motion is accelerated,}$$

and $v = v' - at$ if the motion is retarded.

This shews that a negative acceleration is identical with a retardation, as might have been expected, and henceforth the term acceleration will be supposed to include retardation.

22. The motion of a point, however, may not be uniformly accelerated; and we must find a measure of the acceleration in such a case as this.

Suppose another point whose motion is uniformly accelerated, and let the accelerations on the motion of this and the proposed point be, at the instant under consideration, equal. Then the acceleration on the motion of this point will be measured by the velocity acquired in an unit of time, and therefore the acceleration on the motion of the proposed point will be measured by the velocity which *would* be acquired in an unit of time, supposing the acceleration were to remain constant for that unit of time.

23. If v be the velocity acquired in time t reckoned from the instant under consideration, by means of an acceleration α, and if v' be the velocity which would be acquired in the time t, supposing the acceleration constant, then $\alpha = \dfrac{v'}{t}$; and this is always true, and therefore true in the limit when v' and t are indefinitely diminished.

$$\therefore \ \alpha = \text{Limit } \frac{v'}{t} = \text{Limit } \frac{v}{t}.$$

Δ. 24. By means of the differential calculus we may obtain the same result. For if δv be the velocity acquired in a small time δt immediately subsequent to the instant under consideration, and if α', α'' be the greatest and least values of the acceleration during the time δt, then $\delta v < \alpha'\delta t$ and $> \alpha''\delta t$;

$$\therefore \ \frac{\delta v}{\delta t} < \alpha', \text{ and } > \alpha'',$$

and as α', α'' have the same limit α when δt is indefinitely diminished, we get

$$\frac{dv}{dt} = \alpha.$$

25. This result includes the case of a constant acceleration, for then $\dfrac{v}{t}$ being constant, will $= \text{Limit } \dfrac{v}{t}$ or $= \dfrac{dv}{dt}$.

26. The Parallelogram of Accelerations.

" If two adjacent sides of a parallelogram represent in magnitude and direction two accelerations by which the motion of a point is simultaneously affected, the resulting acceleration will be represented both in magnitude and direction by the diagonal of the parallelogram passing through the point of intersection of those sides."

Let AB, AC represent the two accelerations.

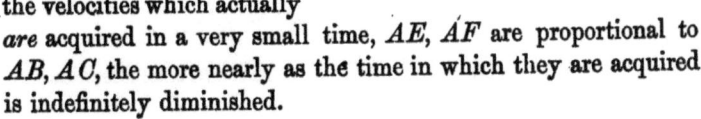

Then AB, AC measure the velocities which would be acquired in an unit of time.

And if AE, AF measure the velocities which actually *are* acquired in a very small time, AE, AF are proportional to AB, AC, the more nearly as the time in which they are acquired is indefinitely diminished.

The resulting velocity will be measured by AG.

The resulting acceleration then must be in the direction of AG and be to AB or AC in the same ratio as AG is to AE or AF respectively; i.e. it will be represented in direction and magnitude by the diagonal AD.

This may be extended to space of three dimensions as was done for velocities in Art. 9, and all the analytical formulæ and remarks of Arts. 10, 11, 12, will equally hold good for accelerations.

27. As we have shewn (Art. 6) how to transform the measure of a velocity from one set of units of space and time to another, we must now shew how to transform the measure of an acceleration.

Let the new units of space and time be a and b times respectively as great as the original units.

Then a, being the measure of the acceleration, is equal to the measure of the velocity acquired in an unit of time; therefore the measure of this velocity, when referred to the new unit of time, will be ba. (See Art. 6.)

But this velocity is *not* acquired in the new unit of time, but only in the bth part of it; therefore the velocity acquired in the new unit of time is b times as great as this, i.e. it $= b^2a$.

This velocity has now to be referred to the new unit of space, and therefore (see Art. 6) its measure is $\dfrac{b'a}{a}$.

This, then, is the measure of the acceleration in terms of the new units.

E. g. If the acceleration on the motion of a point be measured by 20 when a foot and a second are the units, what will be its measure when a yard and a minute are the units?

The velocity acquired in $1''$ is 20 feet per $1''$,

i. e. 20×60 feet per $1'$;

therefore the velocity acquired in $1'$ is $60 \times (20 \times 60)$ feet per $1'$,

$$= \frac{20.60.60}{3} \text{ yards per } 1';$$

therefore the measure of the acceleration is 24,000.

We have purposely chosen the same numbers as those in the transformation of the velocity given in Art. 6, in order that the distinction may be clearly seen. No errour can well arise if it be borne in mind constantly, that the measure of an acceleration is the velocity acquired in an unit of time, estimated *per that unit of time.*

28. All that has been said respecting constant accelerations will equally apply to varying accelerations, by means of considerations analogous to those employed in Art. 17, and by making the necessary changes in phraseology.

CHAPTER II.

29. THE motion of a point in space will be completely determined, if we know the law to which its velocity is subject throughout the motion; and this is usually discovered by knowing the law of the acceleration by which it is affected.

Since the propositions called the parallelogram and parallelepiped of velocities (which equally hold good for accelerations) shew that we may consider that part of the motion which results from any one irrespectively of the others, it will be convenient to resolve the velocity and acceleration into directions at right angles to each other, and to consider them separately.

Δ. 30. We shall now find certain relations between space, time, velocity, and acceleration, here denoted by the letters s, t, v, a.

$$\text{We have } v = \frac{ds}{dt} \text{ (Art. 15),}$$

$$a = \frac{dv}{dt} \text{ (Art. 24);}$$

$$\therefore a = \frac{d^2s}{dt^2}, \text{ if } t \text{ be considered independent variable;}$$

$$\text{or } a = \frac{ds}{dt}\frac{dv}{ds} = v\frac{dv}{ds}, \text{ if } s \text{ be considered independent variable.}$$

The motion has here been supposed rectilinear: if it be curvilinear we shall still have $v = \frac{ds}{dt}$, as may be seen by comparing the motion of a point along a curve with that of one along the tangent, and bearing in mind that the corresponding elements of the arc and tangent are coincident. The other equations cannot be assumed to be true, because the *change* of the velocity is not entirely along the tangent.

Δ. 31. If, in the enunciation of Newton's 10th Lemma, we read "point" instead of "body," and "acceleration" instead of "force," the reasoning still holds good, and we have

$$a = 2 \text{ limit } \frac{s}{t^2}.$$

If t be considered independent variable, this vanishing fraction, being evaluated in the usual way, becomes, after two differentiations, $\frac{d^2s}{dt^2}$, as before obtained.

Δ. 32. If x, y, z be the co-ordinates of the moving point at time t, the cosines of the angles which the direction of the velocity $\frac{ds}{dt}$ makes with the rectangular axes of x, y, z, are

$$\frac{dx}{ds}, \frac{dy}{ds}, \frac{dz}{ds};$$

and therefore (Art. 10) the resolved parts of the velocity in the directions of the axes will be

$$\frac{dx}{dt}, \frac{dy}{dt}, \frac{dz}{dt};$$

and therefore the accelerations in the same directions will be

$$\frac{d^2x}{dt^2}, \frac{d^2y}{dt^2}, \frac{d^2z}{dt^2}. \quad \text{(Art. 30.)}$$

Δ. 33. It is sometimes convenient to consider the position of the moving point as determined by polar co-ordinates.

$$OP = r, \quad POx = \theta,$$

whence $x = r \cos \theta, \quad y = r \sin \theta,$

$$\frac{dx}{dt} = \cos \theta \frac{dr}{dt} - r \sin \theta \frac{d\theta}{dt},$$

$$\frac{dy}{dt} = \sin \theta \frac{dr}{dt} + r \cos \theta \frac{d\theta}{dt},$$

and the velocity in direction of OP

$$= \frac{dx}{dt} \cos \theta + \frac{dy}{dt} \sin \theta = \frac{dr}{dt},$$

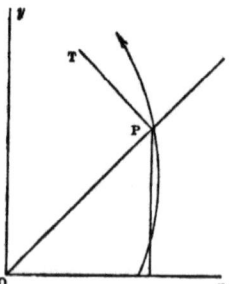

and the velocity in direction PT at right angles to OP, and in direction of the increase of θ,

$$= -\frac{dx}{dt}\sin\theta + \frac{dy}{dt}\cos\theta = r\frac{d\theta}{dt}.$$

Δ. 34. The accelerations may also be obtained in the above directions: for

$$\frac{d^2x}{dt^2} = \cos\theta\frac{d^2r}{dt^2} - 2\sin\theta\frac{dr}{dt}\frac{d\theta}{dt} - r\sin\theta\frac{d^2\theta}{dt^2} - r\cos\theta\left(\frac{d\theta}{dt}\right)^2,$$

and

$$\frac{d^2y}{dt^2} = \sin\theta\frac{d^2r}{dt^2} + 2\cos\theta\frac{dr}{dt}\frac{d\theta}{dt} + r\cos\theta\frac{d^2\theta}{dt^2} - r\sin\theta\left(\frac{d\theta}{dt}\right)^2;$$

therefore the acceleration along OP

$$= \frac{d^2x}{dt^2}\cos\theta + \frac{d^2y}{dt^2}\sin\theta$$

$$= \frac{d^2r}{dt^2} - r\left(\frac{d\theta}{dt}\right)^2{}^*,$$

and the acceleration along PT

$$= -\frac{d^2x}{dt^2}\sin\theta + \frac{d^2y}{dt^2}\cos\theta,$$

$$= 2\frac{dr}{dt}\frac{d\theta}{dt} + r\frac{d^2\theta}{dt^2},$$

$$= \frac{1}{r}\frac{d}{dt}\left(r^2\frac{d\theta}{dt}\right).$$

* The difference in form between these expressions and those for the accelerations in x and y is owing to the fact that the directions of OP, PT are variable, whereas those of x and y are fixed.

That $\frac{d^2r}{dt^2}$ *cannot* represent the acceleration in the direction of OP may be concluded from the consideration of the simple case of motion where r is constant, and ∴ $\frac{d^2r}{dt^2}=0$: but this motion is circular, and there must be an acceleration along the radius, otherwise the point would move in a straight line; therefore when $\frac{d^2r}{dt^2}=0$ there is yet an acceleration existing towards the pole, whence $\frac{d^2r}{dt^2}$ does not express the acceleration in OP as $\frac{d^2x}{dt^2}$ and $\frac{d^2y}{dt^2}$ do those in the directions of x and y. A direct demonstration of these formulæ may be found in Sandeman's treatise *Of the Motion of a Single Particle.*

It must be borne in mind that the positive direction along the radius vector is measured *away* from the pole, and the positive direction at right angles to this is measured in the same direction as that in which θ increases.

Δ. 35. It may be also advantageous to consider the velocity or acceleration as resolved along the tangent and normal.

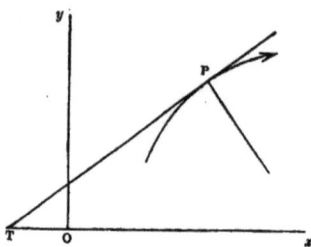

Then we have

$$\cos PTx = \frac{dx}{ds},$$

$$\sin PTx = \frac{dy}{ds},$$

and the velocity in direction of the tangent is $\frac{ds}{dt}$, and that in direction of the normal is 0.

Also the acceleration along the tangent

$$= \frac{dx}{ds}\frac{d^2x}{dt^2} + \frac{dy}{ds}\frac{d^2y}{dt^2},$$

$$= \frac{1}{\frac{ds}{dt}} \cdot \left(\frac{dx}{dt}\frac{d^2x}{dt^2} + \frac{dy}{dt}\frac{d^2y}{dt^2} \right),$$

$$= \frac{1}{2\frac{ds}{dt}} \cdot \frac{d}{dt}\left(\left[\frac{dx}{dt}\right]^2 + \left[\frac{dy}{dt}\right]^2 \right),$$

$$= \frac{d^2s}{dt^2}; \ \because \ \left(\frac{dx}{dt}\right)^2 + \left(\frac{dy}{dt}\right)^2 = \left(\frac{ds}{dt}\right)^2,$$

L.

D

and the acceleration along the normal

$$= \frac{d^2x}{dt^2}\frac{dy}{ds} - \frac{d^2y}{dt^2}\frac{dx}{ds},$$

$$= \frac{1}{\frac{ds}{dt}}\left(\frac{d^2x}{dt^2}\frac{dy}{dt} - \frac{d^2y}{dt^2}\frac{dx}{dt}\right) = \left(\frac{ds}{t}\right)^2 \cdot \frac{1}{\rho} = \frac{v^2}{\rho},$$

if $\rho =$ the radius of curvature*.

The positive directions in this case are measured in the direction of increase of s, and in that which is considered the positive direction of curvature. In the last two sets of resolutions, we have for simplicity considered the motion as taking place in one plane.

Δ. 36. If we know the conditions to which the motion is subject, we can equate the expressions (whether for velocity or acceleration) obtained in the preceding Articles to certain given quantities, and thus obtain sets of differential equations, the solution of which will determine the motion. As the expressions of the preceding Articles have all been derived from those in

---

* These formulæ may be obtained very elegantly in the following manner: let the angle $PTx = \phi$, and let v be the velocity at P, $\left(\text{which} = \frac{ds}{dt}\right)$.

Then the acceleration in x $\quad = \frac{d}{dt}(v \cos \phi) = \cos \phi \frac{dv}{dt} - v \sin \phi \frac{d\phi}{dt}$,

and the acceleration in y $\quad = \frac{d}{dt}(v \sin \phi) = \sin \phi \frac{dv}{dt} + v \cos \phi \frac{d\phi}{dt}$;

∴ the acceleration in TP $\quad = \frac{d^2x}{dt^2}\cos \phi + \frac{d^2y}{dt^2}\sin \phi = \frac{dv}{dt} = \frac{d^2s}{dt^2}$,

and the acceleration along the normal $= \frac{d^2x}{dt^2}\sin \phi - \frac{d^2y}{dt^2}\cos \phi$,

$$= -v\frac{d\phi}{dt} = -v\frac{d\phi}{ds}\cdot\frac{ds}{dt},$$

$$= -v^2 \div \frac{ds}{d\phi},$$

$$= \frac{v^2}{\rho};$$

for as ϕ does not appear except in a differential coefficient, we may increase it by some constant angle, so as to pass to the angle required in the intrinsic equation to the curve: the negative sign has been rejected by considering the direction of the curvature.

Art. 32, these sets of equations are equivalent to one another, and the only advantage of one particular set over another is, that the solution is effected with greater ease. In a few cases, the circumstances of the motion can be determined without the aid of the differential calculus; and we shall now proceed to determine certain particular cases of motion, when possible, without such assistance.

37. Referring to Arts. 4, 14, in which we have $v = \dfrac{s}{t}$ or limit $\dfrac{s}{t}$, we conclude that the measure of a velocity is of 1 dimension in (linear) space, and of -1 in time. Also by Arts. 19, 23, in which $\alpha = \dfrac{v}{t}$ or limit $\dfrac{v}{t}$, the measure of an acceleration is of 1 dimension in velocity, and of -1 in time; and therefore is, on the whole, of 1 dimension in space, and of -2 in time. The measures of space and time of course are of no dimensions in time and space respectively. This evidently accounts for the fact that b^2 appears in the transformation of Art. 27, while b only appears in that of Art. 6, and for a appearing equally in both. The reader would do well to apply these considerations to the analytical expressions in the subsequent Articles, by which many results, that at first sight might appear surprising, will be found to be perfectly consistent: and if they are carefully borne in mind, they will be very useful in preventing errour in any investigation.

CHAPTER III.

38. This is evidently the simplest kind of motion affected by acceleration conceivable, and it will subdivide itself into two heads, according as the direction of the acceleration is or is not coincident with the initial direction of motion.

I. First, then, let the direction of the acceleration be coincident with the direction of motion: here it is plain that the path will be a straight line.

39. If the point move from rest and pass over a space s in time t, the measure of the acceleration being a, then will

$$s = \frac{at^2}{2}.$$

For if we divide the time t into n equal intervals τ, the velocities at the end of these intervals will be

$$a \cdot \tau, \quad a \cdot 2\tau, \quad a \cdot 3\tau, \dots \dots a \cdot n\tau. \quad \text{(Art. 21.)}$$

Suppose now the point to move for each interval τ with the velocity it has at the *end* of that interval: then the whole space passed over would be

$$a\tau \cdot \tau + a \cdot 2\tau \cdot \tau + a \cdot 3\tau \cdot \tau + \dots \dots + a \cdot n\tau \cdot \tau$$

$$= a\tau^2 (1 + 2 + 3 + \dots \dots + n)$$

$$= a\tau^2 \frac{n \cdot (n+1)}{2} = \frac{at^2}{2} \left(1 + \frac{1}{n}\right).$$

Again, suppose the point to move for each interval τ with the velocity it has at the *beginning* of that interval; then the whole space passed over would be

$$0 \cdot \tau + \alpha\tau \cdot \tau + \alpha \cdot 2\tau \cdot \tau + \ldots\ldots + \alpha \cdot (n-1)\,\tau \cdot \tau$$

$$= \alpha\tau^2 \left\{ 0 + 1 + 2 + 3 + \ldots + (n-1) \right\}$$

$$= \alpha\tau^2 \cdot \frac{n\,(n-1)}{2} = \frac{\alpha t^2}{2}\left(1 - \frac{1}{n}\right).$$

But it is manifest that the space *really* passed over must lie between these two magnitudes; and since when n is indefinitely increased, they both become $\frac{\alpha t^2}{2}$, we must have $s = \frac{\alpha t^2}{2}$.

40. The velocity at the end of this time t will be αt (see Art. 21).

Also we shall have by eliminating t, $v^2 = 2\alpha s$.

41. Next, suppose the point t be initially moving with a velocity v'.

Then as the mode of reasoning used in the "parallelogram of velocities" will apply here, we shall have

final velocity = initial velocity + that due to the acceleration,

i. e. $v = v' + \alpha t$.

Also the space passed over = space due to the initial velocity + that due to the acceleration,

i. e. $s = v't + \frac{\alpha t^2}{2}$.

And we shall also have

$$v^2 = v'^2 + 2\alpha t v' + \alpha^2 t^2;$$

$$\therefore v^2 - v'^2 = 2\alpha s.$$

If the motion be retarded, the sign of α is changed.

By means of these equations all the circumstances of the motion are determined.

42. II. The second case will be when the direction of the constant acceleration is not coincident with the initial direction of motion.

Here it is evident that the motion will take place altogether in one plane, viz. that which passes through the initial direction of motion, and that in which the acceleration takes place: let this be the plane of the paper, and let A be the initial position of the moving point, AT the direction of the motion at A, yA the direction of the constant acceleration a, v' the initial velocity which is in direction of AT.

Also let TA make with Ax at right angles to Ay the angle $TAx = \iota$.

Let P be the position of the moving point at any time t reckoned from the beginning of the motion.

Draw TP parallel to yA.

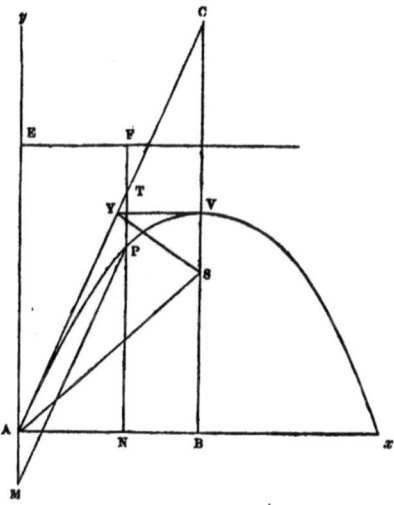

Then we shall have

$$TA = v't.$$

$TP =$ space due to the acceleration

$$= \frac{at^2}{2}.$$

Draw PM parallel to TA meeting yA produced in M; wherefore $TAMP$ is a parallelogram,

$$\text{and}\quad AM = TP = \frac{\alpha t^2}{2} = \frac{\alpha}{2}\left(\frac{TA}{v'}\right)^2$$

$$= \frac{\alpha}{2v'^2}.\,TA^2;$$

$$\text{or}\quad PM^2 = \frac{2v'^2}{\alpha}.\,AM.$$

TA is evidently a tangent to the path at A, therefore the above equation shews that the path is a parabola whose axis is parallel to yA the direction of the acceleration, the concavity being turned in that direction, and the distance of A from the focus $= \dfrac{1}{4}.\left(\dfrac{2v'^2}{\alpha}\right) = \dfrac{v'^2}{2\alpha}.$

43. The position of the focus S is determined as follows:

$$SAB = 90^\circ - SAy = 90^\circ - 2.TAy$$

$$= 90^\circ - 2\,(90^\circ - \iota) = 2\iota - 90^\circ;$$

therefore if CSB be the axis,

$$\left.\begin{array}{l} AB = SA\cos SAB = \dfrac{v'^2}{2\alpha}\sin 2\iota \\[2mm] BS = SA\sin SAB = -\dfrac{v'^2}{2\alpha}\cos 2\iota \end{array}\right\}.$$

As we have drawn the figure $\cos 2\iota$ is negative, $\therefore 2\iota$ is $> 90^\circ.$

44. If V be the vertex, the direction of motion there is parallel to Ax, and therefore the velocity in direction of $Ay = 0$.

Therefore if t' be the time which has elapsed when the moving point reaches V, we must have

$$0 = v'\sin\iota - \alpha t';$$

$$\therefore t' = \frac{v'\sin\iota}{\alpha},$$

and BV will $= BC - CV = AC\sin\iota - CV$

$$= v't'.\sin\iota - \frac{\alpha t'^2}{2} = \frac{v'^2\sin^2\iota}{\alpha 2}.$$

This gives the distance of the vertex V from the line Ax, i. e. shews the greatest positive distance of the moving point from Ax.

45. If L be the latus rectum of the parabola

$$AB^2 = L \cdot BV.$$

$$\therefore L = \frac{AB^2}{BV} = \left(\frac{v'^2}{2a}\sin 2\iota\right)^2 \div \frac{v'^2\sin^2\iota}{2a} = \frac{2v'^2}{a}\cos^2\iota.$$

This might have been obtained in the following manner: If SY be perpendicular to AC,

$$\frac{SV}{SY} = \frac{SY}{SA}, \text{ and } \therefore = \sqrt{\frac{SV}{SA}}.$$

But $\qquad \dfrac{SY}{SA} = \sin(90^\circ - \iota) = \cos\iota; \qquad \therefore \dfrac{SV}{SA} = \cos^2\iota.$

$$\therefore SV = \frac{v'^2}{2a}\cos^2\iota, \text{ or } L = \frac{2v'^2}{a}\cos^2\iota \text{ (see Art. 42)}.$$

46. The distance from A of the other point where the parabola cuts Ax will $= 2AB = \dfrac{v'^2}{a}\sin 2\iota$, and the time which elapses till the moving point takes that position will be

$$\frac{v'^2\sin 2\iota}{a} \div v'\cos\iota = \frac{2v'}{a}\sin\iota.$$

This value might have been obtained by considering that the time in question $= 2 \cdot$ time to vertex $= 2 \cdot \dfrac{v'\sin\iota}{a}$, and the distance from A of the other point where the parabola cuts Ax

$$= 2\frac{v'\sin\iota}{a} \times v'\cos\iota = \frac{v'^2}{a}\sin 2\iota.$$

The directrix of the parabola will be parallel to Ax, and will cut Ay at a point E whose distance from $A = AS = \dfrac{v'^2}{2a}$.

47. The velocity at P in direction Ax will be $v'\cos\iota$, and that in direction Ay will $= v'\sin\iota - at$; therefore if v be this velocity,

$$v^2 = (v'\cos \iota)^2 + (v'\sin \iota - \alpha t)^2$$

$$= v'^2 - 2\alpha v'\sin \iota . t + \alpha^2 t^2$$

$$= 2\alpha . SA - 2\alpha . (TN - TP) \quad \text{(Art. 42)}$$

$$= 2\alpha . (AE - PN)$$

$$= 2\alpha . PF$$

$$= 2\alpha . \text{(distance of } P \text{ from directrix).}$$

Thus the motion is completely determined.

Δ. 48. Both of the foregoing cases of motion may be investigated by the help of the differential calculus, as follows:—

(I) If the acceleration be in the direction of motion, we have

$$\frac{dv}{dt} \text{ or } \frac{d^2s}{dt^2} = \alpha;$$

$$\therefore v \text{ or } \frac{ds}{dt} = \alpha t + C.$$

When $t = 0$, $v = v'$; $\therefore C = v':$

$$\therefore \frac{ds}{dt} \text{ or } v = v' + \alpha t;$$

$$\therefore s = C' + v't + \frac{\alpha t^2}{2}.$$

If s is measured from the initial position of the moving point, then C' will $= 0$, for s and t vanish together. If the moving point be initially at rest, then $v' = 0$.

Also $\alpha = v \dfrac{dv}{ds}$, $\therefore \dfrac{v^2}{2} = C + \alpha s;$

when $s = 0$, $v = v'$, $\therefore C = \dfrac{v'^2}{2};$

and $\therefore v^2 - v'^2 = 2\alpha s.$

L.   E

Δ. 49. (II) If the acceleration be not in the direction of motion we have (using the figure and notation of Art. 42)

$$\frac{d^2x}{dt^2} = 0, \qquad\qquad \frac{d^2y}{dt^2} = -\alpha;$$

$$\therefore \frac{dx}{dt} = C = v' \cos \iota, \qquad \frac{dy}{dt} = C' - at$$

$$= v' \sin \iota - at,$$

since when $t = 0$ the velocities in the directions of x and y are respectively $v' \cos \iota$, $v' \sin \iota$;

$$\therefore x = v' \cos \iota . t, \qquad y = v' \sin \iota . t - \frac{at^2}{2}.$$

(No constants are added in the last integrations,

because x, y, and t all vanish together.)

$$\therefore y = x \tan \iota - \frac{\alpha}{2v'^2 \cos^2 \iota} x^2;$$

$$\therefore \left(x - \frac{v'^2}{2\alpha} \sin 2\iota\right)^2 = \frac{2v'^2 \cos^2 \iota}{\alpha} \left(\frac{v'^2}{2\alpha} \sin^2 \iota - y\right),$$

which shews that the path is a parabola, the co-ordinates of whose vertex are $\frac{v'^2}{2\alpha} \sin 2\iota$, and $\frac{v'^2}{2\alpha} \sin^2 \iota$, whose axis is in the negative direction of y, i. e. in the direction of the acceleration; and whose latus rectum $= \frac{2v'^2 \cos^2 \iota}{\alpha}$.

Δ. CHAPTER IV.*

OF THE MOTION OF A POINT AFFECTED BY AN ACCELERATION, THE DIRECTION OF WHICH ALWAYS PASSES THROUGH A FIXED POINT.

50. This will evidently be of two kinds, according as the initial direction of motion does or does not pass through the fixed point.

(I) Let the initial direction of motion pass through the fixed point, then it is clear that the path is a straight line.

We shall, for simplicity's sake, consider the moving point to be initially at rest at a given position in space.

(j) If the acceleration be constant, the notion is that determined in Arts. 38—41.

51. (ij) Let the acceleration vary as the distance from the fixed point, its direction being towards it.

Take the fixed point for the origin of distance; and let a be the initial distance of the moving point, s its distance, and v its velocity at a time t, reckoned from the beginning of the motion.

The acceleration will be expressed by λs, where $\lambda =$ the measure of the acceleration at distance unity†. The direction of this is from the moving point to the fixed point; therefore if we

---

* Investigations of the results of the Articles in this Chapter, obtained without recourse to the Differential Calculus, will be found in Newton: in all cases the words "force" and "body" should be replaced by "acceleration" and "point".

† N.B. As λs (the acceleration) is of 1 dimension in space and -2 in time, λ must be of no dimensions in space and -2 in time: we should more properly have said that the acceleration at distance unity is measured by λ times the unit of space.

consider the first part of the motion, which is clearly towards the fixed point, we have

$$\frac{d^2s}{dt^2} = -\lambda s,$$

$$\text{or } \left(\overline{\frac{d}{dt}} \middle|^2 + \lambda \right) s = 0;$$

$$\therefore \ s = \left(\overline{\frac{d}{dt}} \middle|^2 + \lambda \right)^{-1} . 0 = A \cos (\sqrt{\lambda} . t + \beta),$$

where A and β are constants, and have to be determined.

We have by differentiation

$$\frac{ds}{dt} \text{ or } v = -\sqrt{\lambda} . A \sin (\sqrt{\lambda} . t + \beta).$$

Then initially $t = 0$, $s = a$, $v = 0$;

$$\therefore \ \beta = 0, \ A = a;$$

and we have $s = a \cos (\sqrt{\lambda} . t)$,

$$v = \div \sqrt{\lambda} . a \sin (\sqrt{\lambda} . t).$$

52. This might have been solved without separating symbols, as follows:

$$\frac{ds^2}{dt^2} = -\lambda s;$$

$$\therefore \ 2 \frac{ds}{dt} \frac{d^2s}{dt^2} = -2\lambda s \frac{ds}{dt};^*$$

$$\therefore \ \left(\frac{ds}{dt} \right)^2 = C - \lambda s^2.$$

Initially, v or $\frac{ds}{dt} = 0$, $s = a$; $\therefore \ C - \lambda a^2 = 0$;

$$\therefore \ \left(\frac{ds}{dt} \right)^2 = \lambda (a^2 - s^2);$$

$$\therefore \ v \text{ or } \frac{ds}{dt} = -\sqrt{\lambda} (a^2 - s^2),$$

---

* It will be easily seen that this multiplication by $\frac{ds}{dt}$ comes to the same thing as transforming $\frac{d^2s}{dt^2}$ into the form $v \frac{dv}{ds}$ in Art. 30.

the negative sign being taken, because the motion is in the negative direction, viz. towards the fixed point;

$$\therefore \sqrt{\lambda} \cdot t + C' = -\int \frac{ds}{\sqrt{a^2 - s^2}}$$

$$= \cos^{-1} \frac{s}{a}.$$

When $t = 0$, $s = a$; $\therefore C' = \cos^{-1} 1$;

$$\therefore s = a \cos (\sqrt{\lambda} \cdot t),$$

and $\dfrac{ds}{dt}$ or $v = - \sqrt{\lambda} \cdot a \sin \sqrt{\lambda} \cdot t$, as before.

53. If we put $s = 0$, we get $t = \dfrac{\pi}{2 \sqrt{\lambda}}$,

$$\text{and } v = - \sqrt{\lambda} \cdot a :$$

this gives the time of reaching the origin and the velocity at that point.

54. The motion now takes place on the negative side of the origin, and will manifestly be the same as if the moving point's velocity $(- \sqrt{\lambda} \cdot a)$ were suddenly reversed, and the motion were on the positive side. Hence, as the law of the acceleration undergoes no change, the velocity will be destroyed in passing over the same space as before, and in the same time, i. e. the moving point will come to rest at a distance a on the negative side of the origin, after the lapse of a time $\dfrac{\pi}{2 \sqrt{\lambda}}$.

Now the moving point is in exactly the same circumstances as it initially was, but on the negative side of the origin: the motion is therefore repeated. Whence it is easily seen that the motion is oscillatory between two points whose distances from the origin are $+ a$ and $- a$, and that the time of a complete oscillation is $4 \cdot \dfrac{\pi}{2 \sqrt{\lambda}} = \dfrac{2\pi}{\sqrt{\lambda}}$, which is independent of the initial position of the moving point. (NEWTON, Prop. 38.)

55. If the point were not initially at rest, its motion may
yet be determined from the case now treated of: for if another
point were to be initially at rest at a distance a' from the origin,
a' may be assumed to be of such magnitude as that, when this
point arrives at the distance a from the origin, it may be moving
with the same velocity as that which the first point initially has,
which we will call v'. Then, by what has been already said,

$$a = a' \cos(\sqrt{\lambda}\,\tau), \quad v' = -\sqrt{\lambda}\,a' \sin(\sqrt{\lambda}\cdot\tau),$$

where τ is the time required for the second point to move from
its initial position (a') to the initial position (a) of the first point.

These two equations will determine a' and τ; and as both
points have the same velocity at the distance a, and also there is
the same acceleration on the motion of both, the subsequent
motions of the two will be identical, and the motion of the first
point will be deduced from the formulæ of the preceding Articles; where it must be borne in mind that the time is reckoned
not from the actual beginning of the motion, but from the beginning of the hypothetical motion of the second point, i. e. that the
time t in the preceding Articles has to be corrected by the
quantity τ.

56. If the direction of the acceleration were away from
the fixed point, we should have

$$\frac{d^2s}{dt^2} = +\lambda s,$$

$$\text{or} \quad \left(\frac{\overline{ds}}{dt}\bigg]^2 - \lambda\right) s = 0;$$

$$\therefore s = A\epsilon^{\sqrt{\lambda}\cdot t} + B\epsilon^{-\sqrt{\lambda}\cdot t};$$

and if the point be initially at rest at a distance a, we should
have

$$a = A + B; \quad 0 = \sqrt{\lambda}\cdot A - \sqrt{\lambda}\cdot B;$$

$$\therefore s = \frac{a}{2}(\epsilon^{\sqrt{\lambda}\cdot t} + \epsilon^{-\sqrt{\lambda}\cdot t}),$$

$$\text{and} \quad \frac{ds}{dt} = v = \sqrt{\lambda}\cdot\frac{a}{2}(\epsilon^{\sqrt{\lambda}\cdot t} - \epsilon^{\sqrt{\lambda}\cdot t}).$$

57. (iij) Let the acceleration vary as the square of the distance from the fixed point inversely, its direction being towards it.

Then with the same notation as before

$$\frac{d^2s}{dt^2} = -\frac{\lambda}{s^2}. \ast$$

Multiplying by $2\frac{ds}{dt}$, and integrating, we have

$$\left(\frac{ds}{dt}\right)^2 = C + \frac{2\lambda}{s}.$$

When $s = a$, $\frac{ds}{dt} = 0$; $\therefore C + \frac{2\lambda}{a} = 0$,

and then $\qquad \frac{ds}{dt} = v = -\sqrt{2\lambda\left(\frac{1}{s} - \frac{1}{a}\right)}$,

taking the negative sign as before (Art. 52);

$$\therefore \sqrt{\frac{2\lambda}{a}}.t = -\int \frac{ds}{\sqrt{\frac{a}{s} - 1}} = -\int \frac{s\,ds}{\sqrt{as - s^2}},$$

$$= -\int \frac{s - \frac{a}{2}}{\sqrt{\frac{a^2}{4} - \left(s - \frac{a}{2}\right)^2}} - \frac{a}{2}\int \frac{ds}{\sqrt{as - s^2}},$$

$$= C' + \sqrt{\frac{a^2}{4} - \left(s - \frac{a}{2}\right)^2} - \frac{a}{2}\,\text{versin}^{-1}\frac{s}{\frac{1}{2}a}.$$

When $t = 0$, $s = a$, and $\therefore C' - \frac{a}{2}\pi = 0$;

$$\therefore t = \sqrt{\frac{a}{2\lambda}}.\left\{\sqrt{as - s^2} + \frac{a}{2}\cos^{-1}.\frac{2s - a}{a}\right\},$$

The time of reaching the origin will be

$$\sqrt{\frac{a}{2\lambda}}.\frac{a}{2}.\pi = \frac{\pi}{2}\sqrt{\frac{a^3}{2\lambda}}.$$

The velocity here will be $-\infty$.

* N.B. λ is of 3 dimensions in space and -2 in time.

58. After this the motion is on the negative side of the origin, and by reasoning similar to that used in the preceding case, the moving point will come to rest at a distance a from the origin, after the lapse of a time $\frac{\pi}{2}\sqrt{\frac{a^3}{2\lambda}}$. It is now in the same circumstances as it initially was, but on the negative side of the origin, and therefore the motion is repeated.

The whole motion is consequently oscillatory between points whose distances from the origin are $+a$ and $-a$, and the time for a complete oscillation

$$= 4\frac{\pi}{2}\sqrt{\frac{a^3}{2\lambda}} = \sqrt{\frac{2}{\lambda}} \cdot \pi a^{\frac{3}{2}}.$$

59. If the motion of the point were supposed not to begin from rest, a similar artifice to that employed in Art. 55, may be made use of here also to determine the motion.

60. Any other such case of motion that may arise is to be investigated in a manner similar to the preceding, by integration of the equation $a = \frac{d^2s}{dt^2}$, or $\frac{dv}{dt}$, or $v\frac{dv}{ds}$; a being given in terms of t, v, or s by the conditions of the problem.

61. (II) Let the initial direction of motion not pass through the fixed point; then it is clear that the path will lie in one plane, which passes through the fixed point and the initial direction of motion.

Let a be the acceleration towards the fixed point taken for origin.

Then if x, y be rectangular co-ordinates, and r, θ polar co-ordinates of the moving point at time t, s the length of path described, v the velocity, and ρ the radius of curvature; we have for the determination of the motion, as the acceleration is entirely *along* the radius vector, (See Arts. 32, 34, 35,)

$$\frac{d^2x}{dt^2} = -\alpha \cos\theta = -\alpha \frac{x}{r}$$
$$\left. \frac{d^2y}{dt^2} = -\alpha \sin\theta = -\alpha \frac{y}{r} \right\} \quad\text{............(1)};$$

or
$$\frac{d^2r}{dt^2} - r\left(\frac{d\theta}{dt}\right)^2 = -\alpha$$
$$\left. \frac{1}{r}\frac{d}{dt}\left(r^2\frac{d\theta}{dt}\right) = 0 \right\} \quad\text{..................(2)};$$

or
$$\frac{d^2s}{dt^2} = -\alpha \frac{dr}{ds}$$
$$\left. \frac{v^2}{\rho} = \alpha\, r\, \frac{d\theta}{ds} \right\} \quad\text{...........................(3)}.$$

Either of these pairs of equations (which are equivalent to each other) will determine the motion.

We shall proceed to investigate some general properties of this kind of motion, and then to discuss more fully its nature in the particular cases of the acceleration varying as the distance, or as the inverse square of the distance, from the fixed point.

62. From the second of equations (2) we get

$$r^2\frac{d\theta}{dt} = h, \text{ a constant.}$$

Now if A be the sectorial area swept out by the radius vector in time t,

$$\frac{dA}{d\theta} = \frac{1}{2}r^2;$$

$$\therefore \frac{dA}{dt} = \frac{h}{2};$$

$$\therefore A = \frac{1}{2}ht,$$

A and t being supposed to begin together; i.e. $A \propto t$, or the area described in any time varies as the time of its description. (NEWTON, Prop. 1.)

L.

F

63. If p be the perpendicular from the origin or pole on the tangent to the path,

$$p\delta s = 2\delta A,$$

the more nearly as δs and δA are more and more diminished;

$$\therefore p = 2\frac{dA}{ds}, \text{ or } p\frac{ds}{dt} = 2\frac{dA}{dt} = h;$$

$$\text{i. e. } pv = h, \text{ or } v = \frac{h}{p}.$$

(NEWTON, Prop. 1, Cor. 1.)

64. As $\dfrac{1}{p^2} = u^2 + \left(\dfrac{du}{d\theta}\right)^2$ where $u = \dfrac{1}{r}$, we shall have

$$v^2 = h^2\left(u^2 + \overline{\frac{du}{d\theta}}\Big|^2\right),$$

which might have been obtained from the formula

$$v^2 = \left(\frac{dr}{dt}\right)^2 + r^2\left(\frac{d\theta}{dt}\right)^2, \text{ (see Art. 33)}$$

by substituting $\dfrac{1}{u}$ for r, and considering that $\dfrac{d\theta}{dt} = hu^2$.

65. From the first of equations (3) we get

$$\frac{d^2s}{dt^2}, \text{ or } v\frac{dv}{ds} = -\alpha\frac{dr}{ds};$$

$$\therefore v^2 = C - 2\int\alpha dr;$$

α being supposed to be a function of r only.

If the initial values of v, r be v', r',

$$v'^2 = C - 2\int_{r'}\alpha dr;$$

$$\therefore v^2 = v'^2 - 2\int_{r'}^{r}\alpha dr.$$

This shews that when the acceleration depends only on the distance from the fixed point, the change of velocity in passing from any one point to any other is dependent only upon the distances of the two positions under consideration, and is independent of the *particular* path described. (NEWTON, Prop. 40.)

66. Also from the second of equations (3)

$$v^2 = a\,\rho r\,\frac{d\theta}{ds}$$

$$= a.\ \{\tfrac{1}{2}\ \text{chord of curvature through the pole}\};$$

$$\therefore\ r\,\frac{d\theta}{ds} = \cos\ (\text{inclination of normal to radius vector}).$$

Now if a point be moving from an initial position of rest, its motion being affected by a *constant* acceleration a, the direction of which is always the same; and if s_1 be the space described when the point's velocity is v, we shall have (by Art. 40)

$$v^2 = 2a\,s_1\,;$$

$$\therefore\ s_1 = \tfrac{1}{4}\ (\text{chord of curvature}).$$

s_1 is called the space due to the velocity v: and it must be borne in mind that for this case the acceleration is supposed to be continued constant for the requisite time with the magnitude (a) which it has at the instant under consideration. (NEWTON, Prop. 6, Cor. 4).

67. To determine the path we shall find equations (2) most convenient.

We have, putting $\dfrac{1}{u}$ for r,

$$r^2\,\frac{d\theta}{dt} = h\ \text{ or }\ \frac{d\theta}{dt} = hu^2,$$

$$\frac{dr}{dt} = -\frac{1}{u^2}\frac{du}{d\theta}\frac{d\theta}{dt} = -h\frac{du}{d\theta},$$

$$\frac{d^2r}{dt^2} = \frac{d}{d\theta}\left(-h\frac{du}{d\theta}\right)\frac{d\theta}{dt}$$

$$= -h\frac{d^2u}{d\theta^2}\,.\,hu^2\,;$$

$\therefore$ substituting in the equation $\dfrac{d^2r}{dt^2} - r\left(\dfrac{d\theta}{dt}\right)^2 = -\alpha,$

we have $- h^2u^2 \dfrac{d^2u}{d\theta^2} - \dfrac{1}{u} \cdot h^2u^4 = -\alpha,$

or $\dfrac{d^2u}{d\theta^2} + u = \dfrac{\alpha}{h^2u^2}.$

The solution of this equation determines the path.

68.   We shall now proceed to discuss the particular cases mentioned above; and

(j)   Let the acceleration vary as the distance from the fixed point.

Then $\alpha = \dfrac{\lambda}{u};$

$\therefore \dfrac{d^2u}{d\theta^2} + u = \dfrac{\lambda}{h^2u^3},$

$\therefore 2\dfrac{du}{d\theta}\dfrac{d^2u}{d\theta^2} + 2u\dfrac{du}{d\theta} = \dfrac{2\lambda}{h^2u^3}\dfrac{du}{d\theta},$

$\therefore \left(\dfrac{du}{d\theta}\right)^2 + u^2 = C - \dfrac{\lambda}{h^2u^2};$ ....(a)

$\therefore \left(\dfrac{du}{d\theta}\right)^2 = \dfrac{1}{u^2}\left(Cu^2 - \dfrac{\lambda}{h^2} - u^4\right),$

$\therefore \dfrac{du}{d\theta} = -\dfrac{1}{u}\sqrt{Cu^2 - \dfrac{\lambda}{h^2} - u^4};$

taking the negative sign for convenience;

$\therefore \theta = \beta - \displaystyle\int \dfrac{u\,du}{\sqrt{Cu^2 - \dfrac{\lambda}{h^2} - u^4}}$

$= \beta - \dfrac{1}{2}\displaystyle\int \dfrac{d\cdot\left(u^2 - \dfrac{C}{2}\right)}{\sqrt{\left(\dfrac{C^2}{4} - \dfrac{\lambda}{h^2}\right) - \left(u^2 - \dfrac{C}{2}\right)^2}}$

$= \beta + \dfrac{1}{2}\cos^{-1}\cdot\dfrac{u^2 - \dfrac{C}{2}}{\sqrt{\dfrac{C^2}{4} - \dfrac{\lambda}{h^2}}}.$

If we had taken the positive sign above, the only difference would have been that β would have been changed.

$$\therefore u^2 = \frac{C}{2} + \sqrt{\frac{C^2}{4} - \frac{\lambda}{h^2}} \cos 2(\theta - \beta) \dots\dots\dots\dots(b).$$

69. We must now determine C, β, and h.

If the point be moving initially with a velocity v' in a direction inclined at an angle ι to the prime radius vector r', then $v'r' \sin \iota = h$, which is therefore known.

Also in (a) we have the left-hand side $= \dfrac{v'^2}{h^2}$, (Art. 64);

$$\therefore \frac{v'^2}{h^2} = C - \frac{\lambda}{h^2} r'^2;$$

$$\therefore C = \frac{1}{r'^2 \sin^2 \iota} + \frac{\lambda}{v'^2 \sin^2 \iota};$$

this determines C.

As $\theta = 0$ initially, we have

$$\frac{1}{r'^2} = \frac{C}{2} + \sqrt{\frac{C^2}{4} - \frac{\lambda}{h^2}} \cos 2\beta,$$

which gives β.

70. The equation (b) shews that the orbit is an ellipse whose center is at the pole, and the angle vector of its apse* is β.

If the acceleration were in the opposite direction, the sign of λ would be changed, and the equation (b) would represent an hyperbola whose center is at the pole†.

---

* By an "*apse*" is meant any point in the curve where the radius vector is perpendicular to the tangent. In the ellipse, for example, when the origin is the center, the extremities of the axes are apses; if the focus were the origin, the extremities of the major axis only are apses.

† This case of motion may be easily solved in the following manner.

We have the acceleration in $x = -\lambda r \cos \theta = -\lambda x$, and that in $y = -\lambda r \sin \theta = -\lambda y$, supposing its direction to be always *towards* the origin ;

71. It may be convenient to obtain a value for C in terms of the axes of the ellipse.

therefore $\dfrac{d^2x}{dt^2} + \lambda x = 0$, and $\dfrac{d^2y}{dt^2} + \lambda y = 0$.

$\therefore$ as in Art. 51, $x = A\cos(\sqrt{\lambda}.t - \beta)$, and $y = A'\cos(\sqrt{\lambda}.t - \beta')$,

where A, A', β, β', are certain constants.

Between these 2 equations t must be eliminated.

The result is clearly $\cos^{-1}\dfrac{x}{A} - \cos^{-1}\dfrac{y}{A'} = \beta' - \beta$:

take the cosine of each side and write C for $\cos(\beta' - \beta)$.

Then $\dfrac{x}{A}.\dfrac{y}{A'} + \sqrt{1 - \dfrac{x^2}{A^2}}.\sqrt{1 - \dfrac{y^2}{A'^2}} = C$;

$$\therefore 1 - \frac{x^2}{A^2} - \frac{y^2}{A'^2} + \frac{x^2y^2}{A^2A'^2} = \left(C - \frac{xy}{AA'}\right)^2;$$

$$\therefore \frac{x^2}{A^2} + \frac{y^2}{A'^2} - 2C.\frac{xy}{AA'} = 1 - C^2,$$

which is a conic section whose center is at the origin.

To determine whether it is an ellipse or an hyperbola we have

$$\left(-\frac{2C}{AA'}\right)^2 - 4\frac{1}{A^2}.\frac{1}{A'^2} = -\frac{4}{A^2A'^2}(1 - C^2),$$

which is negative, $\therefore$ C, being $= \cos(\beta' - \beta)$, is < 1;

$$\therefore \text{ the path is an ellipse.}$$

If the direction of the acceleration were *away* from the origin, then we should have

$$\frac{d^2x}{dt^2} - \lambda x = 0, \quad \text{and} \quad \frac{d^2y}{dt^2} - \lambda y = 0;$$

$$\therefore x = Ae^{\sqrt{\lambda}.t} + A'e^{-\sqrt{\lambda}.t}, \quad \text{and} \quad y = Be^{\sqrt{\lambda}.t} + B'e^{-\sqrt{\lambda}.t};$$

$$\therefore B'x - A'y = (AB' - A'B)e^{\sqrt{\lambda}.t}, \quad \text{and} \quad Bx - Ay = (A'B - AB')e^{-\sqrt{\lambda}.t};$$

$$\therefore BB'x^2 + AA'y^2 - (A'B + AB')xy = -(A'B - AB')^2.$$

And as $(A'B + AB')^2 - 4BB'.AA'$, which $= (A'B - AB')^2$, is positive, the path is an hyperbola.

If these be 2a and 2b,

as $u^2 = \frac{1}{2}\left\{\frac{1}{a^2} + \frac{1}{b^2} + \left(\frac{1}{a^2} - \frac{1}{b^2}\right) \cos 2\,(\theta - \beta)\right\}$,

we have from (b)

$$\frac{1}{a^2} + \frac{1}{b^2} = C, \text{ and } \frac{1}{a^2} - \frac{1}{b^2} = \sqrt{C^2 - \frac{4\lambda}{h^2}};$$

$$\therefore \left(\frac{1}{a^2} - \frac{1}{b^2}\right)^2 = \left(\frac{1}{a^2} + \frac{1}{b^2}\right)^2 - \frac{4\lambda}{h^2};$$

$$\therefore \frac{\lambda}{h^2} = \frac{1}{a^2 b^2};$$

$$\therefore C = \frac{a^2 + b^2}{a^2 b^2} = \frac{\lambda}{h^2}(a^2 + b^2).$$

72. Substituting this value of C in the equation (a), we obtain

$$(\text{velocity})^2 = \lambda\,(a^2 + b^2 - r^2),$$

$$= \lambda\,(\text{semi-conjugate diameter})^2.$$

73. This might have been obtained without reference to (b); thus:

If v_1, v_2, be the velocities at the extremities of a and b,

$$v_1 a = h = v_2 b \quad (\text{Art. 63});$$

also from (a) $\left.\begin{array}{l} v_1^2 = h^2 C - \lambda a^2 \\ v_2^2 = h^2 C - \lambda b^2 \end{array}\right\}$, $\because r = a, b$, respectively.

Then we have $\dfrac{v_1^2}{b^2} = \dfrac{v_2^2}{a^2} = \dfrac{v_1^2 + v_2^2}{b^2 + a^2} = \dfrac{2h^2 C - \lambda(a^2 + b^2)}{a^2 + b^2}$;

also each $= \dfrac{v_2^2 - v_1^2}{a^2 - b^2} = \dfrac{\lambda(a^2 - b^2)}{a^2 - b^2}$;

$\therefore$ by equating these we get $\dfrac{2\,h^2 C}{a^2 + b^2} - \lambda = \lambda,$

or $h^2 C = \lambda (a^2 + b^2);$

$\therefore$ (velocity)$^2 = h^2 C - \lambda r^2 = \lambda (a^2 + b^2 - r^2),$ as before.

74. The axes of the ellipse are determined by the conditions

$$a^2 + b^2 = \frac{h^2}{\lambda}\, C = \frac{v'^2\, r'^2 \sin^2 \iota}{\lambda}\left(\frac{1}{r'^2 \sin^2 \iota} + \frac{\lambda}{v'^2 \sin^2 \iota}\right),$$

$$= \frac{v'^2}{\lambda} + r'^2,$$

and $a^2 b^2 = \dfrac{h^2}{\lambda} = \dfrac{v'^2\, r'^2 \sin^2 \iota}{\lambda}.$

The first of these might have been got at once from the results of the last two Articles.

75. For the determination of the period, i. e. the time required to describe the whole ellipse, we have

$$\frac{h}{2}\ (\text{period}) = \text{area of ellipse} \ (\text{Art. 62});$$

$$\therefore \text{period} = \frac{2\pi ab}{\sqrt{\lambda a^2 b^2}} = \frac{2\pi}{\sqrt{\lambda}},$$

which is independent of the form of the ellipse, and is therefore the same for all ellipses described under accelerations subject to the same law as above, and of the same magnitude at all equal distances. (NEWTON, Prop. 10.)

76. (ij) Let the acceleration vary as the inverse square of the distance from the fixed point.

Then $\alpha = \lambda u^2;$

$$\therefore \frac{d^2 u}{d\theta^2} + u = \frac{\alpha}{h^2 u^2} = \frac{\lambda}{h^2};$$

$$\therefore u = \left(1 + \overline{\frac{d}{d\theta}\Big|}^2\right)^{-1} \cdot \left(\frac{\lambda}{h^2}\right) + \left(\overline{\frac{d}{d\theta}\Big|}^2 + 1\right)^{-1} \cdot (0),$$

$$= \frac{\lambda}{h^2} + A \cos(\theta - \beta),$$

$$\text{or } \frac{h^2}{\lambda} u = 1 + \frac{Ah^2}{\lambda} \cos (\theta - \beta).$$

This is the equation to a conic section whose focus is at the pole, the angle vector of the apse being β, the latus rectum $\dfrac{2h^2}{\lambda}$, and the eccentricity $\dfrac{Ah^2}{\lambda}$; and therefore it is an ellipse, parabola, or hyperbola, according as $\dfrac{Ah^2}{\lambda}$ is $< = $ or > 1.

77. This might have been obtained, as in Art. 52, by putting

$$u - \frac{\lambda}{h^2} = w, \text{ whence } \frac{d^2 w}{d t^2} + w = 0;$$

$$\therefore w = A \cos (\theta - \beta).$$

78. We have also

$$\left(\frac{du}{d\theta}\right)^2 + u^2 = A^2 \sin^2 (\theta - \beta) + \left\{\frac{\lambda}{h^2} + A \cos (\theta - \beta)\right\}^2$$

$$= \frac{\lambda^2}{h^4} + A^2 + \frac{2\lambda}{h^2} A \cos (\theta - \beta);$$

$\therefore$ (by Art. 64)

$$(\text{velocity})^2 = \frac{\lambda^2}{h^2} + A^2 h^2 + 2\lambda A \cos (\theta - \beta)$$

$$= 2\lambda u - \left(\frac{\lambda^2}{h^2} - A^2 h^2\right).$$

79. The constants A, β, and h, are determined by the initial circumstances of the motion, viz. by the following equations:

$$\left. \begin{array}{c} \dfrac{h^2}{\lambda} \cdot \dfrac{1}{r'} = 1 + \dfrac{Ah^2}{\lambda} \cos \beta \\[2ex] v'^2 = \dfrac{2\lambda}{r'} - \left(\dfrac{\lambda^2}{h^2} - A^2 h^2\right) \\[2ex] v' r' \sin \iota = h \end{array} \right\},$$

using the notation of Art. 69.

L.

G

80. If a be the semiaxis major of the conic section, and e the eccentricity,

$$a(1 - e^2) = \text{semi-latus rectum}$$

$$= \frac{h^2}{\lambda}$$

and $e = \dfrac{Ah^2}{\lambda}$, (Art. 76).

$$\therefore a = \frac{h^2}{\lambda} \cdot \frac{1}{1 - \dfrac{A^2h^4}{\lambda^2}} = \frac{1}{\dfrac{\lambda}{h^2} - \dfrac{A^2h^2}{\lambda}};$$

$$\therefore (\text{velocity})^2, \text{ which} = 2\lambda u - \lambda\left(\frac{\lambda}{h^2} - \frac{A^2h^2}{\lambda}\right)$$

$$= \frac{2\lambda}{r} - \frac{\lambda}{a};$$

whence also $\dfrac{1}{a} = \dfrac{2}{r} - \dfrac{v^2}{\lambda}$,

which is independent of the initial direction of motion;

and $b^2 = a^2(1 - e^2) = a \cdot \dfrac{h^2}{\lambda}$

$$= a \cdot \frac{v'^2 r'^2 \sin^2 \iota}{\lambda}$$

$$= \frac{v'^2 r'^2 \sin^2 \iota}{\dfrac{2\lambda}{r'} - v'^2}.$$

81. The expression $v^2 = \dfrac{2\lambda}{r} - \dfrac{\lambda}{a}$ might have been obtained thus:

multiplying the equation $\dfrac{d^2u}{d\theta^2} + u = \dfrac{\lambda}{h^2}$ by $2\dfrac{du}{d\theta}$ and integrating, we have

$$\left(\frac{du}{d\theta}\right)^2 + u^2 = \frac{2\lambda}{h^2}u - C,$$

or $(\text{velocity})^2 = 2\lambda.u - h^2 C;$

∴ if v_1, v_2, be the velocities at the extremities of the major axis,

$$\left.\begin{array}{c} v_1 \cdot (1+e) \cdot a = h = v_2 \cdot (1-e) \cdot a, \\[2mm] v_1^2 = \dfrac{2\lambda}{a\,(1+e)} - h^2 C, \\[2mm] v_2^2 = \dfrac{2\lambda}{a\,(1-e)} - h^2 C. \end{array}\right\}$$

$$\therefore \frac{2\lambda}{a}(1+e) - h^2 C (1+e)^2 = \frac{2\lambda}{a}(1-e) - h^2 C \cdot (1-e)^2 ;$$

$$\therefore \frac{2\lambda}{a} \cdot 2e = h^2 C \cdot 4e,$$

$$\text{or } h^2 C = \frac{\lambda}{a} ;$$

$$\therefore (\text{velocity})^2 = 2\lambda u - \frac{\lambda}{a} = \frac{2\lambda}{r} - \frac{\lambda}{a}.$$

82. In the two preceding Articles the conic section has been treated as if it were an ellipse: if e were > 1, i.e. if it were an hyperbola, we should have $a\,(e^2-1) = $ semi-latus rectum; the only effect this has is to change the sign of a: then we shall have

$$v^2 = \frac{2\lambda}{r} + \frac{\lambda}{a}.$$

If e were $= 1$, i.e. if the curve were a parabola, we should have

$$v^2 = \frac{2\lambda}{r}.$$

83. $\quad e^2 = \dfrac{A^2 h^4}{\lambda^2} = \dfrac{h^2}{\lambda^2}\left(v'^2 - \dfrac{2\lambda}{r'} + \dfrac{\lambda^2}{h^2}\right)$ (Art. 79).

$$= \frac{v'^2 h^2}{\lambda^2} - \frac{2h^2}{\lambda r'} + 1$$

$$= \frac{v'^4 r'^2 \sin^2 \iota}{\lambda^2} - \frac{2 v'^2 r' \sin^2 \iota}{\lambda} + 1$$

$$= 1 + \frac{v'^2 r' \sin^2 \iota}{\lambda^2}\{v'^2 r' - 2\lambda\},$$

which is $\gtrless 1$, according as $v''^2 \gtrless \dfrac{2\lambda}{r'}$;

i.e. according as the space due to the initial velocity, which (see Art. 66) $= \dfrac{v'^2}{\frac{2\lambda}{r'^2}}$, is $\gtrless r'$.

84. If the path be an ellipse, the period will be

$$\frac{2\pi ab}{h} = \frac{2\pi ab}{\sqrt{\dfrac{\lambda . b^2}{a}}};$$

$$\because \frac{b^2}{a} = \tfrac{1}{2}\text{ latus rectum} = \frac{h^2}{\lambda};$$

$$\therefore \text{ the period} = \frac{2\pi}{\sqrt{\lambda}} a^{\frac{3}{2}}.$$

85. If in the preceding cases the direction of the acceleration had been *away* from the fixed point, the sign of a would have been changed, and the motion would be determined in an exactly similar manner: if we change the sign of λ in the two preceding cases of motion, the equation (b) of Art. 68 would determine the path to be an hyperbola, in which

$$\frac{1}{a^2} - \frac{1}{b^2} = \frac{C}{2}, \text{ and } \frac{1}{a^2} + \frac{1}{b^2} = \sqrt{\frac{C^2}{4} + \frac{\lambda}{h^2}},$$

and the equation of Art. 76 would become

$$\frac{h^2}{\lambda} u = -1 + \frac{Ah^2}{\lambda} \cos(\theta - \beta),$$

which represents an hyperbola, because by Art. 83, e would then be always > 1. (NEWTON, Props. 11—15).

86. The equation $\dfrac{d^2u}{d\theta^2} + u = \dfrac{a}{h^2 u^2}$ may be made use of to determine the law of variation of the acceleration towards a fixed point, in order that the moving point may trace out a given curve.

For a relation is given between u and θ, from which we obtain $\dfrac{d^2u}{d\theta^2}$, and then $\alpha = h^2u^2\left(\dfrac{d^2u}{d\theta^2} + u\right)$ gives α, which is usually required in terms of u.

E.g. Let the given curve be an ellipse: the acceleration being towards the center.

Then $u^2 = \dfrac{\cos^2\theta}{a^2} + \dfrac{\sin^2\theta}{b^2}$,

$$= \frac{1}{2}\left(\frac{1}{a^2} + \frac{1}{b^2}\right) + \frac{1}{2}\left(\frac{1}{a^2} - \frac{1}{b^2}\right)\cos 2\theta; \quad \ldots\ldots(1)$$

$$\therefore \; u\frac{du}{d\theta} = -\frac{1}{2}\left(\frac{1}{a^2} - \frac{1}{b^2}\right)\sin 2\theta;$$

$$\therefore \; u\frac{d^2u}{d\theta^2} + \left(\frac{du}{d\theta}\right)^2 = -\left(\frac{1}{a^2} - \frac{1}{b^2}\right)\cos 2\theta. \quad \ldots\ldots(2)$$

Also $u^2\left(\dfrac{du}{d\theta}\right)^2 = \dfrac{1}{4}\left(\dfrac{1}{a^2} - \dfrac{1}{b^2}\right)^2(1 - \cos^2 2\theta)$

$$= \frac{1}{4}\left(\frac{1}{a^2} - \frac{1}{b^2}\right)^2 - \left\{u^2 - \frac{1}{2}\left(\frac{1}{a^2} + \frac{1}{b^2}\right)\right\}^2$$

$$= \left(\frac{1}{a^2} + \frac{1}{b^2}\right)u^2 - u^4 - \frac{1}{a^2b^2}. \quad \ldots\ldots\ldots(3)$$

Also from (1) and (2), we get

$$u\frac{d^2u}{d\theta^2} + 2u^2 + \left(\frac{du}{d\theta}\right)^2 = \frac{1}{a^2} + \frac{1}{b^2};$$

$$\therefore \; u\left(\frac{d^2u}{d\theta^2} + u\right) = \frac{1}{a^2} + \frac{1}{b^2} - u^2 - \left(\frac{du}{d\theta}\right)^2$$

$$= \frac{1}{a^2b^2}u^{-2}, \text{ from (3)};$$

$$\therefore \; \alpha = h^2u^2\left(\frac{d^2u}{d\theta^2} + u\right) = \frac{h^2}{a^2b^2}u^{-1}$$

$$= \lambda \cdot \text{(distance)}, \text{ where } \lambda = \frac{h^2}{a^2b^2}.$$

The velocity at any point will $= h \sqrt{u^2 + \left(\frac{du}{d\theta}\right)^2}$, (Art. 64.)

$$= h \sqrt{u^2 + \left(\frac{1}{a^2} + \frac{1}{b^2} - u^2 - \frac{1}{a^2 b^2} u^{-2}\right)}, \text{ from (3),}$$

$$= h \sqrt{\frac{1}{a^2} + \frac{1}{b^2} - \frac{r^2}{a^2 b^2}}$$

$$= \sqrt{\lambda (a^2 + b^2 - r^2)}$$

$$= \sqrt{\lambda}. \text{ (semi-diameter conjugate to } r),$$

as before, (Art. 72).

For an hyperbola we have only to write $- b^2$ for b^2, and we get a similar result, the only difference being that the sign of λ is changed, i. e. that the direction of the acceleration is *away* from the fixed point.

87. Next, let the given curve be a conic section, the acceleration being always towards the focus.

$$\text{Then } \frac{c}{r} = 1 + e \cos\theta,$$

$$\text{or } u = \frac{1 + e \cos\theta}{c},$$

where $c =$ the semi-latus rectum, and $e =$ the eccentricity;

$$\therefore \frac{d^2 u}{d\theta^2} = - \frac{e \cos\theta}{c};$$

$$\therefore a = h^2 u^2 \left(\frac{d^2 u}{d\theta^2} + u\right) = \frac{h^2}{c} u^2$$

$$= \lambda \text{ (distance)}^{-2}, \text{ where } \lambda = \frac{h^2}{c}.$$

And the velocity at any point $= h \sqrt{u^2 + \left(\frac{du}{d\theta}\right)^2}$

$$= h \sqrt{\left(\frac{1 + e \cos\theta}{c}\right)^2 + \left(\frac{e \sin\theta}{c}\right)^2}$$

$$= h \sqrt{\frac{1 + e^2 + 2e \cos \theta}{c^2}}$$

$$= \sqrt{\lambda \cdot \frac{1 + e^2 + 2e \cos \theta}{c}}$$

$$= \sqrt{\frac{2\lambda}{r} - \frac{\lambda}{a}}, \text{ as before, (Art. 80).}$$

88. In these and other like cases of motion, the time of describing any part of the path will be found from the equation

$$r^2 \frac{d\theta}{dt} = h,$$

or $ht = \displaystyle\int_{\theta_1}^{\theta_2} r^2 d\theta,$

where θ_1, θ_2 are the values of θ at the beginning and end of the time of description that is under consideration, and r is determined in terms of θ from the equation

$$\frac{d^2u}{d\theta^2} + u = \frac{a}{h^2 u^2}.$$

89. Any other cases of motion that may arise are investigated in a similar manner: the most general equations being

$$\frac{d^2x}{dt^2} = a_x; \quad \frac{d^2y}{dt^2} = a_y; \quad \frac{d^2z}{dt^2} = a_z;$$

where $a_x a_y a_z$ represent the resolved parts of the acceleration in the directions of the co-ordinate axes. The particular artifices to be used for the solution will of course depend on the forms in which $a_x a_y a_z$ appear.

90. In investigating any motion, if we use tangential and normal resolutions, so that our equations of motion are (see Art. 35) $\dfrac{d^2s}{dt^2} = a$, and $\dfrac{v^2}{\rho} = a'$, the former expression (which is equivalent to $\dfrac{dv}{dt} = a$, or $v\dfrac{dv}{ds} = a$) is only concerned for the

instant with changing the magnitude of the velocity without altering its direction; while the other, without causing any instantaneous alteration in its magnitude, changes its direction. This normal acceleration may be taken to measure the tendency to proceed in a straight line. It is sometimes called centrifugal acceleration: the term is not a good one, because the direction of a' is estimated *towards* the center of curvature, not *from* it; but whenever this, or any other equivalent term is used, let the reader know that $\dfrac{v^2}{\rho}$ is all that is meant.

CHAPTER V.

OF MATTER AND FORCE.

91. WE have hitherto considered motion in itself, irrespectively of any cause: we shall now consider it with reference to the cases of nature, and apply the foregoing articles to the solution of such questions as may arise.

It will be necessary to make some remarks on the different class of ideas that will now be called up in the mind. All ideas with which we are here concerned are formed upon observation or upon experiment: to the former class rigid mathematical reasoning can be applied, but not to the latter, at least to any extent; owing to the fact that in the former kind all adventitious circumstances attending the formation of the idea can at once be detected by the mind and separated from what is necessary to such formation, but in the latter case they cannot: indeed, doubts may arise as to whether any such circumstance is really adventitious or necessary. The idea of space or extension, whether linear, superficial, or solid; the idea of time or succession of events, and those of number and magnitude, are obtained from observation. From experiments on things in the natural world we obtain the ideas of matter and force, of which we shall say more hereafter. The evidence of experiment is, so to speak, not so independent of ourselves as that of observation, and therefore the conclusions we draw from the ideas obtained from the former are not so abstractedly true as those drawn from the other kind of ideas. For example, the theorems of geometry, which merely depend on the idea of space, and the theorems relating to numbers, are so true that it is impossible to conceive any other circumstances existing under which they should cease to be true; but any conclusions obtained from experiments, which of course involve the nature of the things experimented upon, are not so: in fact, it is quite possible to

L.

H

imagine that circumstances may exist under which they will be false.

92.   We shall not attempt to define matter and force, because no satisfactory definition can be given; we shall however make some remarks on the distinction between material and immaterial things, and on the connection of force with matter.

If we *observe* objects around us, we immediately obtain the idea that they possess finite extension and a certain form: this is no more than the idea of a geometrical figure. But by *experimenting* we find another property existing in them all; viz. that if we take two of them and endeavour to make one occupy any of the space taken up by the other, it is necessary first to displace this: in other words, that no two such things can occupy the same space at the same time.   This property is called impenetrability.   The possession of this property then, is that which fundamentally distinguishes a material thing (or a "body," as it is called) from a geometrical figure: for two geometrical figures can always be made to coincide, or occupy the same space at the same time, as, for instance, the two triangles in Euclid I. 4; also a geometrical figure can be made to coincide with a material body, as a shadow cast from an opaque body does with any object that may be situated in it, as far as it goes.

93.   Another idea that is called up in the mind by the same experiment of displacing, in the case when the displacement is made in order that a man's hand may occupy the space taken up by any material body, is that of force or exertion required to perform this displacement.   The ideas of force and matter are therefore necessarily connected, and cannot be considered in mathematical reasoning without reference to each other; in other words, the action of force follows from the possession of impenetrability.   These ideas cannot be obtained by any amount of observation whatever.

94.   But motion was defined in Art. 1 to be change of position in space, and it was said that all motion had reference to space and time: it may further be said that the idea of

motion involves no other ideas than those of space and time: it belongs therefore to the class of ideas obtained from observation alone, which may be called geometrical ideas; and, consequently, the conclusions that have been arrived at in the preceding chapters (seeing that motion has been treated geometrically in them) are as true as any other geometrical propositions; and therefore will be more abstractedly true than the propositions in the subsequent articles, which will involve the ideas of matter and force.

95. It was stated above that the idea of force is obtained from the experiment of a body being displaced by ourselves. We can conclude, as before, that our own bodies consist of matter, and as we also perceive that force is called into action merely by the bodies possessing impenetrability, we are able to generalize this notion, and infer that force is exerted when the displacement is made by any other material body than our own.

However many experiments may be made on things in the world around us, they all call up the same ideas of matter and force as those above described, and no other. Force may clearly be looked upon in two ways: (1) that exertion we experience when we displace a material body; (2) that unknown something which goes on between us and that body, or between two bodies when one is displaced by the other (caused by the fact that both possess impenetrability), owing to which the displacement is effected. These of course are connected together, but the latter is the only way in which force will be regarded.

The idea of the *existence* of force then is got from its displacing, and therefore causing motion in, a material body; another experiment enables us to conclude that force will change the motion of a body that already is in motion. Since in performing the experiments above mentioned we sometimes experience more exertion and sometimes less, it is clear that one force may be greater than another.

These ideas however are but vague; and in order to get a clearer notion, a force must be estimated by what it will just do, or what it will just not do, which is much the same thing. We shall, then, by means of experiments relating to forces (for observations cannot be made here), and by making necessary conventions regarding the measures thereof, be able to make our propositions depend on geometrical or algebraical truths.

96. All our experiments on matter lead us to conclude that it is purely passive and does not of itself change its condition, but requires a force to act upon it to do so. Now it is observed that all material bodies will, if placed at rest and allowed to be free, fall towards the earth, but that this can be prevented by the action of a force: we infer then that it is a force which would cause all bodies to fall towards the earth. This force is called weight or gravity: a certain body is taken and the weight of it is called 1 lb.: the force which is to be exerted so as just to prevent it from falling is called a force of 1 lb.; another such body would require another force of 1 lb. to support it, and the two together would require a force which would be called 2 lbs., and so on. This is the only method on which forces can be measured. And as this supposes a state of rest in the bodies on which they act, all investigations regarding forces as such must be pursued under the hypothesis of their producing rest; the science which treats of forces then is Statics. In works on this subject will be found a convention of representing forces by straight lines, and a law of force, the truth of which rests solely on experiment, viz. that the point of application of a force may be transferred to any point in its line of action without altering the effect. From these is deduced the proposition called "the parallelogram of forces," and then the whole science is reduced into a geometrical science, to which of course the ordinary reasonings will apply. Thus after the above law and convention are taken for granted, we find that the resolved part of a force F in a direction inclined at an angle θ to its direction is $F \cos \theta$, simply because the length of the side of a rectangular parallelogram inclined at an angle θ to its diagonal $=$ length of diagonal $\times \cos \theta$; and for no other reason. The experimental laws then are for the purpose of getting rid of forces; and in all statements respecting forces that occur in Statics the word "force" may be replaced by the word "line."

97. We shall now treat of the effect of forces when causing motion in material bodies. The science which refers to this is

called Dynamics. It must be remembered that it is only in material bodies this takes place, for in the motion of a shadow, or in that of a ghost (which in popular belief possesses finite extension and capability of motion, but is without impenetrability), no force can act at all. The science of motion being a purely geometrical one, though force be the cause of motion in material bodies, it will be necessary for us in this case also to ascertain certain experimental laws by which we may get rid of force, and reduce Dynamics into the geometrical science of motion, in a similar manner to that in which Statics is reduced into Geometry.

98. A quantity of matter of the smallest possible dimensions is called a particle, and may be regarded approximately as like a geometrical point. The fundamental proposition by which the motion of a particle is determined is the following:—

If a material particle and a geometrical point be initially coincident in space, and be moving with the same velocity in the same direction, and if forces act on the particle so as to change its velocity in the same way as that of the point is changed, then the particle and the point will *always* be coincident in space.

This is obviously axiomatic; and hence the motion of the particle is deduced from that of the point, which can be determined by the methods of the foregoing chapters. From this we shall see that the proposition called "the parallelogram of velocities" will be true for a particle, though the reasoning used in Art. 8 to prove it will not hold good, owing to the fact that the particle cannot be compelled to move along the line AB (see the figure of Art. 8), except under the application of a force to compel it: we cannot then conclude that that hypothesis will properly represent the motion of the particle.

99. Since the effect of a force is to produce or change motion, i. e. to generate velocity, and therefore to produce an acceleration, the laws we must seek for must be to connect the measures of the forces in any case with those of the accelerations they produce: these can only be determined by experiment. They ought to be obtained from the most simple cases, and

therefore the forces ought to be supposed to act on material particles: we can consequently make approximate experiments only, from a number of which we draw our conclusions regarding the laws. Their truth is established in the following manner: (1) an hypothesis is taken which is *a priori* probable, as far as we can judge; (2) experiments are made in which the conditions of the hypothesis are approximately satisfied, and observations are taken by which we see that the more nearly the above conditions are satisfied, the more nearly does the result agree with what we should expect it to be; (3) calculations are made of complicated cases of motion, under the assumption of the truth of the hypothesis, and the result of calculation is found to agree with the case of nature. The next chapter will be devoted to the discussion of these laws.

CHAPTER VI.

OF THE DYNAMICAL LAWS OF FORCE, COMMONLY CALLED,
THE LAWS OF MOTION.

100. IN investigating the connection between forces and the motions produced, it will be clearly necessary and sufficient to obtain definite statements on the three following points: (1) the general effect of a force on a particle: (2) what that effect is: (3) when there are several particles influencing each other's motion, what connection there is between the forces called into action. We shall therefore have three laws of motion. It will be necessary to have a law to satisfy us on the first point, because force does not admit of a satisfactory definition, as the idea of it is got from experiment. The formal statement on this point must then be taken together with our notions of force, thus supplying the place of a definition.

The idea of force was that it caused or changed motion. The first law of motion then will be for the purpose of setting forth this idea definitely, i.e. stating a necessary connection (under the present state of nature) between force and motion in material bodies: this is best done negatively, by considering the state of the case where no force acts. If there is such a necessary connection, no motion will then be caused, or if the particle be in motion, its motion will not be changed; therefore it will either be at rest, or move in a straight line with uniform velocity. Since forces that statically balance each other have no resultant, the same ought to be true when the particle is supposed to be acted upon by forces in statical equilibrium.

101. THE FIRST LAW OF MOTION then will be:—"If a material particle be acted upon by no external force, or by

forces which statically balance each other, it will either be at rest, or be moving uniformly in a straight line."

102. We shall now have to test the truth of this by experiments.

(1) If the particle be at rest it will remain at rest.

This is a reasonable hypothesis from the ideas we have of the passive nature or inertia of matter; for there seems to be no reason why a body at rest should begin to move in any one direction rather than any other: moreover, in all cases when a body at rest begins to move, we find from experience that some force has always acted to cause this motion.

(2) If the particle be in motion it will proceed in a straight line.

There is *a priori* no reason why it should deviate on one side rather than another. And in all cases of curvilinear motion we find that external forces act. If a stone be thrown in a direction inclined to the vertical, its path is curved; but the force of weight has been continually acting which would make the position of the stone at any instant lower than what it would otherwise be. When a stone is thrown along the ground, supposed horizontal, its path is nearly straight; and considering the asperities and unevennesses of the surface, there will be a number of forces called into action at the stone's contact with them, that *may* account for its deviation from a rectilinear path: moreover, the more we do away with these forces, which is done by making the surface smoother, the more nearly do we find the path become a straight line, thus leading us to suppose that the above forces *do* account for the deviation. When a carriage in motion is suddenly turned to one side, a person in it feels a tendency towards the other side of the carriage, i.e. to proceed in space in the same direction as before.

(3) If the particle be in motion its velocity is constant.

There is *a priori* no reason why of itself the particle should increase its velocity rather than diminish it, or *vice versâ*. And we find from experience that when the velocity is changed, forces have acted: for example, in the case of the stone thrown along the ground, the velocity certainly is diminished, but this may be due to the friction and the resistance of the air: and it is also found that the more these are diminished, as in the case of a smooth level sheet of ice, the less is the diminution of the velocity. If a carriage in motion be suddenly stopped, a person in it is thrown forward, i. e. his body has a tendency to proceed with its previous motion.

From such experiments as the above we conclude that the first Law of Motion is true.

103. Having settled that the invariable effect of a force is motion, we proceed to inquire *what* motion does a force cause? To obtain an answer that we may expect to be true, we must consider that the idea of force is one in itself, whether force be considered statically or dynamically: therefore the special properties of force must be intrinsically the same in both subjects. These have been investigated in Statics: therefore we must state them now in a dynamical form. The special properties are the following: that a force is independent of any particular point in its line of action; that it is independent, as far as regards its line of action, of any other force (this latter is got from the parallelogram of forces): and as time is not involved in Statics, because we have there not instantaneous but permanent rest, that force is also independent of time.

From this we should infer that the special dynamical properties of a force would be that its effect is independent of any velocity already existing (for that only depends on space and time); and independent, as far as regards its own direction, of any other force. If with these we combine the consideration of the measure of a force arising from the addition of units, we should expect the effect of a force, i. e. the acceleration it produces, to be proportional to its magnitude.

104. We state all this in the following manner as

THE SECOND LAW OF MOTION.

"When any number of forces act on a material particle, the acceleration which any one of them produces on the motion is the same, both in direction and magnitude, as if it had acted on

L.   I the particle at rest, and the other forces had not acted at all, being proportional to the intensity of the force."

105. In establishing the truth of this, we find (1) that a force acting constantly in the same direction and with the same intensity on a particle at rest, will produce an uniformly accelerated motion in its own direction. As an example of such a force we may take the weight of the body, which acts always vertically downwards, and is the same for all moderate heights above the earth's surface; therefore if our statement is true, the motion of a body dropped from rest ought to be uniformly accelerated. If observations be made on such motions, it is found that they very nearly agree with what they ought to be, and the resistance of the air seems quite sufficient to account for the discrepancy.

If a body were let fall down an inclined plane, the force on it would be its weight × sine of the inclination of the plane to the horizon, and therefore is constant, and the motion ought to be of the same kind as before. This motion is easier to observe than the preceding, because by diminishing the inclination of the plane the acceleration may be made small, but there is friction as well as the resistance of the air to cause a discrepancy.

(2) The same is true if the particle have an initial motion in the direction in which the force acts.

This may be tested by observing the motion of a body thrown vertically upwards, or that of a body projected directly up or down an inclined plane; and we can also investigate whether the acceleration in this case is the same as in the preceding: we find that it is so, and hence conclude that the effect of a constant force is independent of any velocity in its own direction.

(3) This is also true if the body have a velocity in any other direction.

As an example of such motion we may take the case of a body projected in a direction not vertical: then we ought to have the case of a point whose motion is affected by a constant acceleration vertically downwards, and equal to the acceleration due to its weight (Art. 42), and therefore the path of such a body ought to be a parabola whose axis is vertical, and con-cavity downwards. The resistance of the air will of course cause a deviation from this motion, but the deviation is so small as to lead us to conclude that this statement is true. This might also be tested on an inclined plane, as in the two former cases. From all this it appears that the effect of a force is independent of any velocity the body may have.

(4) The accelerations produced by constant forces are pro-portional to their intensities.

If a body of weight W be placed successively on two planes inclined to the horizon at angles ι, ι', then the forces which cause its motion are in the respective cases $W\sin\iota$, $W\sin\iota'$; therefore if this statement be true, the accelerations of the mo-tion in these cases are in the ratio of $W\sin\iota$: $W\sin\iota'$, i. e. $\sin\iota$: $\sin\iota'$, or if the planes be of the same length, in the ratio of their heights. This can easily be tested from observations of the motions; and it may be observed that the friction may be made very small, and if the inclinations of the planes be small, the velocity of the body will never be very great, so that the resistance of the air will have much less effect than if the body were moving with a great velocity, and the observations on the motion can be more conveniently taken.

(5) If any number of constant forces act in the same di-rection, the acceleration produced will be equal to the sum of the accelerations which they would separately produce.

Let the forces be F_1, F_2, &c. and the accelerations they would separately produce be α_1, α_2, &c.; also let F be the result-ing force, and α the acceleration produced by it.

Then F is in the same direction as F_1, F_2, &c., and therefore α is in the same direction as α_1, α_2, &c.

Also, by the preceding case,

$$\frac{F}{\alpha} = \frac{F_1}{\alpha_1} = \frac{F_2}{\alpha_2} = \&c.,$$

and therefore each $= \dfrac{F_1 + F_2 + \ldots}{\alpha_1 + \alpha_2 + \ldots}$.

But $F = F_1 + F_2 + \ldots$; $\therefore$ $\alpha = \alpha_1 + \alpha_2 + \ldots$

From this it appears that we can correctly obtain the motion by considering the component forces, taking their effects separately, and then combining them.

(6) The effect of any constant force acting on a particle is independent of *any other* constant force that may be acting.
Let AB, AC represent two constant forces in direction and
magnitude, then completing the
parallelogram BC, their resultant is represented by AD.

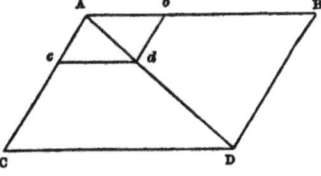

The acceleration produced will consequently be in the direction of AD, and let it be represented by Ad.

Draw db, dc parallel to DB, DC.

Then $Ab : Ac : Ad :: AB : AC : AD$; and therefore Ab, Ac represent the accelerations due to AB, AC. Whence it appears that we may take the separate effects of the component forces and combine them by the parallelogram of accelerations, and thus correctly investigate the motion. This can be extended to more than two forces, after the manner of Art. 9.

(7) The foregoing statements will also be true for *any* forces.

For the effect of a variable force at the instant in question will be measured by the effect of an equal force continued constant for a certain time, and therefore the measures of the accele-
rations will be the same (for the instant) as if the forces were continued constant, and consequently will be subject to the above laws. On this plan the truth of the Second Law of Motion is established.

106. We have yet to determine the coefficient of the pro-
portionality between the measures of a force and the acceleration

produced by it: this evidently depends on the nature of the particle acted upon, for the same force acting upon different particles is found to produce different accelerations.

It is evident that if any number of particles be taken with equal quantities of matter in them, the same force must be exerted on each to make them move in the same way: and if they be connected together, the effect of the above system of forces will not be altered: i. e. if F be the force acting on each particle to produce an acceleration α in its motion, there being n particles; when they are connected together, or formed into one particle, all the forces, i. e. nF, must act in order to produce the same acceleration α as before. Now the quantity of matter in this last particle is n times as great as the quantity of matter in one of the original particles: wherefore, in order that the accelerations on different particles may be the same, the intensity of the forces acting on them must be proportional to the quantity of matter in the particles. This is the only plan on which we can proceed to estimate the quantity of matter in bodies. The measure of the quantity of matter in a body is called its mass.

107. The force then acting on a particle varies as the acceleration produced as long as the mass of the particle is the same, and as the mass when the acceleration is the same; therefore generally the force varies as the mass of the particle and the acceleration produced jointly; i. e. if forces F, F' acting on particles whose masses are M, M', produce accelerations α, α', then $\dfrac{F}{F'} = \dfrac{M}{M'} \cdot \dfrac{\alpha}{\alpha'}$. We must assume the unit of mass: let the mass of the second particle M' be the unit of mass, then

$$\frac{F}{F'} = \frac{M}{1} \cdot \frac{\alpha}{\alpha'}, \text{ or } M = \frac{\alpha'}{\alpha} \cdot \frac{F}{F'}.$$

F', α' are at present undetermined: let them both $= 1$,

$$\text{then } M = \frac{F}{\alpha} \text{ or } F = M\alpha.$$

This assumption fixes the unit of mass to be that quantity of matter in which the unit of force produces the unit of accele-

ration, and then we have the numerical measure of the intensity
of a force equal to the product of the numerical measures of the
mass moved and the acceleration produced.

108. The mass of a body is proportional to its weight, for
the acceleration of gravity is the same on all bodies, as is
established by the experiment of letting fall at the same instant
two bodies of very different weights, such as a sovereign and a
feather from the same height within the exhausted receiver of an
air-pump, when they are found to reach the bottom at the same
instant. Therefore, as the accelerations on these are equal, the
force causing motion is proportional to the mass moved (Art.
106), i. e. the mass of a body is proportional to its weight.

109. The expression Ma is called the moving or motional
effect of a force, and $M \times$ (the measure of the velocity) is called
the momentum or quantity of motion of a body. Also $M \times$ (velocity)^2 is called the *vis viva* of the body.

110. It now remains to determine what effects particles produce on the motion of each other, and we must be guided by
the analogous case in Statics, which is that of bodies pressing
against each other, or exerting forces by means of strings or
rods: in this case the forces exerted by any two particles are
equal in magnitude and opposite in direction, and we should
therefore expect the same to hold good in Dynamics. Since
under the conventions we have adopted the intensity of the
force is measured by the product of the measures of the mass
and the acceleration, i. e. by the motional effect, we state in the
following manner

The Third Law of Motion.

" If one particle act on another particle, the motional effect
produced by the first on the second is equal in magnitude and
opposite in direction to that produced by the second on the first."
Or concisely thus: "Action and reaction are equal and opposite."

111. We may test this by observing the motion of two bodies of different weights hanging by a fine inextensible string over a pulley.

Let W, W' be the weights of the bodies, $(W > W')$, and g the acceleration due to gravity, i. e. the acceleration of motion in a body falling freely under its own weight. Also let T be the tension of the string; then the force downwards on the heavier particle' is $W - T$, and that upwards on the other is $T - W'$, if the law be true. Now on the motion of the heavier particle the force W, and on the other the force W', produces an acceleration g, therefore (by Art. 105, (4)) the accelerations on these are respectively

$$\frac{W - T}{W} \cdot g, \qquad \frac{T - W'}{W'} \cdot g *.$$

But the string being always stretched, the downward motion of the heavier particle is identical with the upward motion of the other, and consequently the above accelerations are equal,

$$\text{i. e. } \frac{W - T}{W} g = \frac{T - W'}{W'} g,$$

and therefore each of these $= \dfrac{W - W'}{W + W'} g$.

This is the acceleration on the motion of each particle; and as it is a constant acceleration, the motion possesses the properties investigated in Arts. 39, 40, 41. In making experiments we can see whether these properties are possessed in any case, and as it is found that they are, we conclude that the law is true.

* If M, M' be the masses of the particles, these accelerations can be represented by $g - \dfrac{T}{M}, \dfrac{T}{M'} - g.$ (Art. 107.)

112. This motion is shewn in a machine called from its inventor Atwood's Machine, which consists of a graduated pillar, on the top of which is a pulley whose axis rests on wheels in order to diminish friction. *A* is a small stage which can be fixed at any point along the graduated scale. The machine is furnished with clockwork, having a pendulum vibrating seconds or half seconds. The weights of the bodies being known, the acceleration

$$\frac{W-W'}{W+W'}g$$

can be computed, and thence the space passed over in any time. If the body *M* be let fall from the highest graduation, and the stage *A* be fixed at the computed distance, after the assigned time has elapsed the body strikes *A*, as nearly as possible.

To test the magnitude of the velocity a ring *B* is adjusted in the same manner at the stage *A* : the difference between the weights is caused by a bar resting on *M*, which is too long to pass through the ring *B*, while *M* itself will do so. The ring is fixed at the point where *M* passes after a certain time from the beginning of the motion, and the velocity of *M* is calculated at that time: there being now no acceleration on it (as the extra weight of the bar is taken off by the ring) the motion is uniform, and the place *M* ought to arrive at after any time is calculated: the stage *A* is fixed there, and *M* is found to strike it at the proper time as nearly as possible. The near agreement of these and other experiments with the cases of computation leads us to conclude that the Laws of Motion are true: hence in any case we reason that the acceleration actually produced on the motion of the particle is that which the particular force produces, and *no other;* and therefore we substitute for the intensity of the force, its motional effect, and then pass to the acceleration; wherefore the motion becomes the same as that of a *point* under certain accelerations, which we have dealt with in the preceding chapters.

CHAPTER VII.

113. (j) FALLING BODIES. A body falling freely towards the earth is acted on by its weight: this is the only force in action, the resistance of the air being neglected; its intensity is constant, and its direction always vertically downwards, therefore the acceleration it produces is constant and always in the same direction, and therefore the motion is the same as that of a point under a constant acceleration in an unvarying direction, which has been determined in Arts. 38—41 and Art. 48; the case of a body projected vertically upwards or vertically downwards is also included. In these cases we must put for the acceleration a, that due to gravity, which is usually denoted by the symbol g, and which has, by means of experiments on pendulums, been found to be 32·2 feet per second, nearly.

114. Then we have, in the case of a body let fall from rest, if s be the space passed over in time t, and at that instant the velocity be v,

$$\left.\begin{array}{l} s = \tfrac{1}{2}gt^2 \\ v = gt \\ v^2 = 2gs \end{array}\right\} \ldots (\text{Arts. 39, 40}).$$

If the body be projected vertically downwards with a velocity V,

$$\left.\begin{array}{l} s = Vt + \tfrac{1}{2}gt^2 \\ v = V + gt \\ v^2 = V^2 + 2gs \end{array}\right\} \ldots (\text{Art. 41}).$$

If the body be projected vertically upwards with a velocity V,

$$\left.\begin{array}{l} s = Vt - \tfrac{1}{2}gt^2 \\ v = V - gt \\ v^2 = V^2 - 2gs \end{array}\right\} \ldots (\text{Art. 41}).$$

115. In the last case we see that the body will rise until $v = 0$, and then will return: the time of its ascent will be $\dfrac{V}{g}$, and the height through which it will have ascended will be $\dfrac{V^2}{2g}$: it will have arrived again at the point from which it was projected when $s = 0$, i.e. when $t = \dfrac{2V}{g}$, and then its velocity $= -V$; therefore the times of the ascent and descent are equal, and the motion in them is exactly reversed.

116. (ij) PROJECTILES. This case is that of a heavy body projected in a direction inclined to the vertical. Neglecting the resistance of the air, the only force acting is the weight of the body vertically downwards. By the Second Law of Motion the direction of the acceleration this produces is vertically downwards, and its magnitude is not affected by the velocity of the body, and therefore it is g, as in the preceding case: consequently the motion is the same as that of a point when the acceleration is constant and always in the same direction, the initial motion being in another direction. This has been determined in Arts. 42—47, and Art. 49, and in them α must be replaced by g.

117. The path is a parabola whose axis is vertical and concavity downwards. If V be the initial velocity, and the initial direction of motion be inclined at the angle ι to the horizon, the distance of the focus from the point of projection will be $\dfrac{V^2}{2g}$, (Art. 42): its co-ordinates (measured horizontally and vertically upwards from the point of projection) will be

$$\frac{V^2}{2g}\sin 2\iota, \quad -\frac{V^2}{2g}\cos 2\iota \text{ (Art. 43)}:$$

the height of the vertex will be $\dfrac{V^2 \sin^2 \iota}{2g}$ (Art. 44); this is the highest point in the path of the projectile: the height of the directrix (which is horizontal) $= \dfrac{V^2}{2g}$ (Art. 46):

the latus rectum $= \dfrac{2V^2}{g}\cos^2 \iota$ (Art. 45): the range of the pro-jectile (by which is meant the distance between the point of projection and the point where it strikes the ground, considered to be a horizontal plane) will be $\dfrac{V^2}{g}\sin 2\iota$, and the time of flight will be $\dfrac{2V}{g}\sin \iota$ (Art. 46).

The velocity at any point

$$= \sqrt{2g \times \text{(distance of that point from the directrix)}}$$

= velocity acquired by a body initially at rest falling freely from the directrix to that point (Arts. 47, 40).

The position at any time t from the commencement of the motion is determined by the equations

$$\left.\begin{array}{l} x = V\cos \iota \,.\, t \\ y = V\sin \iota \,.\, t - \dfrac{gt^2}{2} \end{array}\right\},$$

when x and y are measured horizontally and vertically upwards from the point of projection.

118. (iij) Rectilinear Motion about a Center of Force.—Here the force is supposed to vary according to any law, and therefore, as by the Second Law of Motion the acceleration produced varies directly as the intensity of the force, it will also vary according to the same law as that to which the force is subject. We will confine ourselves to the case where the force varies as the distance from the center in which it is supposed to be situated, or as the (distance)$^{-2}$; therefore the acceleration will also vary as the distance, or as the (distance)$^{-2}$.

It was observed (Art. 105) that the weight of a body is sensibly the same at moderate distances above the Earth's surface; but at greater distances the supposition that its weight (which is caused by the Earth's attraction) varies as the (distance)$^{-2}$ from the center of the Earth, is more correct; and within the Earth's surface, as in the case of deep mines, the weight is more correctly supposed to vary directly as the distance from the center of the Earth. Both these suppositions may be deduced from the law of universal gravitation, i.e. that every particle of matter attracts every other particle with a force producing an acceleration which varies as the mass of the attracting particle, and inversely as the square of the distance between them.

Δ. 119.   Then (1) if the force vary as the distance, we have the acceleration $\alpha = \lambda$ (distance): this motion is determined in Arts. 51—54.

The results there obtained are

$$\left. \begin{aligned} s &= a \cos (\sqrt{\lambda}\, t) \\ v &= - \sqrt{\lambda} \cdot a \sin (\sqrt{\lambda}\, t) \end{aligned} \right\};$$

the time t being reckoned from the commencement of the motion, and the body being initially at rest at a distance a from the center of force, and being at a distance s from it at the end of the time t.

The body will make oscillations between points equally distant from the center of force; and the time of a complete oscillation is $\dfrac{2\pi}{\sqrt{\lambda}}$. If the body were not initially at rest, the artifice used in Art. 55 might be employed.

Δ. 120.   (2) Let the force vary inversely as the square of the distance: therefore the acceleration $= \lambda$ (distance)$^{-2}$: this motion has been determined in Arts. 57—59, the results of which are, supposing the body initially at rest,

$$\left. \begin{aligned} v &= - \sqrt{2\lambda \left(\frac{1}{s} - \frac{1}{a} \right)} \\ t &= \sqrt{\frac{a}{2\lambda}} \left\{ \sqrt{as - s^2} + \frac{a}{2} \cos^{-1} \frac{2s - a}{a} \right\} \end{aligned} \right\}.$$

The motion will be oscillatory, as in the former case; the time of a complete oscillation being $\sqrt{\dfrac{2}{\lambda}} \cdot \pi a^{\frac{3}{2}}$.

121.* (iv) CURVILINEAR MOTION ABOUT A CENTER OF FORCE.—Here the direction of the acceleration will always pass through a fixed point, and therefore the motion is that investigated in Arts. 61—85; the general properties of this kind of motion will be found in Arts. 62—66. If we suppose the force to be attractive and to vary as the distance or as (distance)$^{-2}$, the acceleration will be towards the center, and will vary according to the same law.

122. If the acceleration $= \lambda$ (distance), the motion is that discussed in Arts. 68—75; the path being an ellipse whose center is the center of force: the period of revolution is $\dfrac{2\pi}{\sqrt{\lambda}}$ (Art. 75); therefore all bodies revolving about a common center of force varying as the distance describe their elliptic orbits in the same time, of whatever dimensions these orbits may be.

123. If the acceleration $= \lambda$ (distance)$^{-2}$, the motion is that discussed in Arts. 76—85: the path is a conic section (generally an ellipse), and the center of force is in the focus. In the case of the ellipse the period of revolution is $\dfrac{2\pi}{\sqrt{\lambda}} a^{\frac{3}{2}}$ (Art. 84); whence if a number of bodies describe ellipses about a common center of force varying as the (distance)$^{-2}$, the squares of their periods of revolution vary as the cubes of the major axes of their orbits, i. e. as the cubes of their mean distances from the center of force.

124. In all these cases, when the acceleration is known, the force acting on the body in motion at any instant can be ascertained, by multiplying the numerical measure of the acceleration by the numerical measure of the mass of the body (Art. 107).

125. KEPLER'S LAWS.—The motion of the planets in their orbits about the Sun were discovered by Kepler to be subject to the three following laws;

* If the reader be unacquainted with the Differential Calculus, he will find the results of the following Articles established in Newton, sect. ij. iij.

' (j) That each planet describes an ellipse about the Sun, which is situated in the focus thereof.

(ij) That the sectorial areas swept out by the line joining the planet and the Sun in all equal intervals of time are equal.

(iij) That the squares of the periods of any of the planets about the Sun vary as the cubes of their mean distances from it.

126. From the second of these laws we have the sectorial area swept out in any time $\propto$ time of describing it; therefore if the Sun be taken for origin of polar co-ordinates, and A be the sectorial area described in time t, $A = Ct$, where C is a constant;

$$\therefore \frac{dA}{d\theta} \text{ or } \tfrac{1}{2} r^2 = C \frac{dt}{d\theta};$$

$$\therefore r^2 \frac{d\theta}{dt} = 2C;$$

$$\therefore \frac{1}{r} \frac{d}{dt} \left(r^2 \frac{d\theta}{dt} \right) = 0;$$

whence, by Art. 34, there is no acceleration perpendicular to the radius vector, or the whole acceleration is along the radius vector; wherefore the whole force on any one planet is constantly directed towards the Sun. (NEWTON, Prop. 2.)

127. From the first law, compared with Art. 87, it will appear that the acceleration on the motion of any one planet varies as the (distance)$^{-2}$ from the Sun, or that the force on any planet varies as the (distance)$^{-2}$.

128. From the third law, if we take any two planets whose orbits have a, a' for their semi-major axes, the absolute accelerations[*] on them being λ, λ',

$$a^{\frac{3}{2}} : a'^{\frac{3}{2}} :: \text{period of first planet} : \text{period of second}$$

$$:: \frac{2\pi}{\sqrt{\lambda}} a^{\frac{3}{2}} : \frac{2\pi}{\sqrt{\lambda'}} a'^{\frac{3}{2}}, \quad \text{(Art. 84)}.$$

[*] By the absolute acceleration is meant the acceleration at distance unity.

whence $\lambda' = \lambda$, or the absolute accelerations on all the planets are equal; therefore, if they were all placed at the same distance from the Sun, the accelerations on them all would be the same.

129. It appears then that on the motion of the planets the force is central, varying as $(\text{distance})^{-2}$, and producing an acceleration independent of the particular planet under discussion: we most reasonably conclude that this force resides in the Sun, i. e. that the planets move under the Sun's attraction only. This at first sight militates against the law of universal gravitation, but more delicate observations have shewn that these laws are not rigidly true, but very nearly so: and the fact that the mass of any of the planets is very small, compared with that of the Sun, would lead us to expect that this would be the case if the law of universal gravitation were true.

CHAPTER VIII.

OF CONSTRAINED MOTION OF PARTICLES.

130. In these cases certain geometrical conditions are required to be satisfied, and unknown forces are involved arising from the constraint; these produce unknown accelerations; and the method pursued to determine the motion is deduced from the consideration, that if external forces be applied continually equal to the forces arising from the constraint, the cause of constraint may be withdrawn, and the motion is unaltered: this then becomes the case of free motion under some unknown forces but with some known conditions, i. e. the motion of a point under some unknown accelerations but with some known geometrical properties.

131. To determine the motion of a heavy particle down a smooth inclined plane.

Let W be the weight of the particle;

R the normal pressure on the plane, which by the Third. Law of Motion = the reaction of the plane on the particle;

g, ξ, the accelerations due to these respectively;

ι the inclination of the plane to the horizon.

Then we have $\dfrac{W}{R} = \dfrac{g}{\xi}$ by the Second Law of Motion (Art. 105 (4)).

And if a force continually equal to R be made to act constantly on the particle, in the direction from the plane to it, the plane may be removed, and the motion is free and the same as the constrained motion under consideration.

Then the force in the direction down the plane $= W \sin \iota$;

and the force perpendicular to the plane $= W \cos \iota - R$:

therefore the acceleration down the plane $= g \sin \iota$,

and the acceleration perpendicular to the plane $= g \cos \iota - \xi$.

But since there is no motion perpendicular to the plane, we must have

$$g \cos \iota - \xi = 0.$$

And the acceleration down the plane, being $g \sin \iota$, is constant, and therefore the motion is that determined in Arts. 38—41, where α is to be replaced by $g \sin \iota$.

Since $g \cos \iota - \xi = 0$, and $\dfrac{W}{R} = \dfrac{g}{\xi}$, we shall have $R = W \cos \iota$; giving the pressure on the plane, which we see is of constant intensity throughout the motion.

If the particle had initially any velocity not directly up or down the plane, the motion would be parabolic, as in Arts. 42—47, wherein α will $= g \sin \iota$.

132. In the motion directly down an inclined plane, we have

$$v^2 - v'^2 = 2 \cdot g \sin \iota \cdot s \text{ (Art. 41)}$$
$$= 2g (s \sin \iota),$$

where v is the final velocity, viz. that at B,

v' the initial velocity, at A,

s the space passed over, viz. AB.

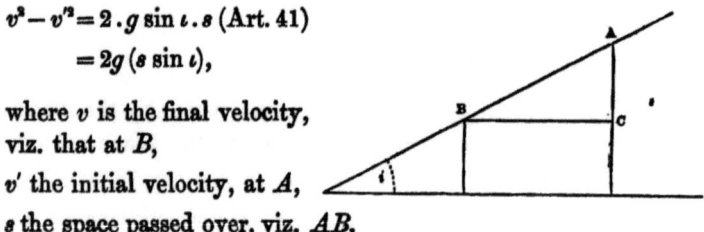

Draw BC horizontal and AC vertical.

Then $AC = AB \sin \iota = s \sin \iota$;

$$\therefore v^2 - v'^2 = 2g \cdot AC.$$

This is the same formula as that for a heavy body falling *freely* through a space AC, which is the difference of the heights of the two positions of the body in the case in question. The above reasoning will also apply if the motion be up the plane. This is generally cited thus: that the change of velocity is due to the vertical space through which the body has descended or ascended, irrespective of the inclination of the plane.

L.

L

133. In a heavy body falling down a smooth plane curve this same property holds good.

For the curve may be considered to arise from a series of indefinitely small inclined planes, AB, BC, CD, DE, &c., each being inclined at the same acute angle (say θ) to the next.

Draw AL vertical, and Bb, Cc, Dd, Ee, &c. horizontal.

Let v' be the velocity at A,

$v_1 =$ that at B on the plane AB;

$\therefore v_1 \cos \theta =$ that at B on the plane BC:

$v_2 =$ the velocity at C on the plane BC,

$v_3 =$ that at D on the plane CD,

&c. ;

and let $v =$ the final velocity, at a point in the same horizontal line with L.

$$\text{Then } v_1^2 - v'^2 = 2g \cdot Ab,$$
$$v_2^2 - (v_1 \cos \theta)^2 = 2g \cdot bc,$$
$$v_3^2 - (v_2 \cos \theta)^2 = 2g \cdot cd,$$
$$\&\text{c.}$$
$$v^2 - (v_n \cos \theta)^2 = 2g \cdot kL ;$$

therefore, by addition,

$$v^2 - v'^2 + (v_1^2 + v_2^2 + \ldots + v_n^2) \sin^2 \theta = 2g \cdot AL.$$

If ϕ be the whole deflection from the direction of motion at A, $\phi = n\theta$.

And $(v_1^2 + v_2^2 + \ldots + v_n^2) \sin^2 \theta$ is essentially a positive quantity, and $< nV^2 \sin^2 \dfrac{\phi}{n}$, V being the greatest of the quantities $v_1, v_2 \ldots v_n$;

$$\therefore (v_1^2 + v_2^2 + \ldots + v_n^2) \sin^2 \theta \text{ is } < V^2 \left(\frac{\sin \dfrac{\phi}{n}}{\dfrac{\phi}{n}} \right)^2 \cdot \frac{\phi^2}{n}.$$

Now if n be indefinitely increased, the limit of $\dfrac{\sin \frac{\phi}{n}}{\frac{\phi}{n}}$ is 1,

(ϕ being expressed in circular measure);

$\therefore (v_1^2 + v_2^2 + \ldots + v_n^2) \sin^2 \theta$ is a positive quantity less than one that becomes indefinitely small, and therefore it vanishes.

Whence $\qquad v^2 - v'^2 = 2g \cdot AL,$

and AL is the vertical space descended.

134. The times of descent of a heavy body initially at rest down all chords of a vertical circle through the highest or lowest points are the same.

Let A be the lowest point of a circle, and let t be the time of descent down any chord AC.

Also let AB be the diameter, and the angle $BAC = \theta$.

Then the force down AC is $W \cos \theta$, and therefore the acceleration is $g \cos \theta$;

$\therefore AC = \tfrac{1}{2} g \cos \theta \cdot t^2$ (Art. 39);

$$\therefore t = \sqrt{\frac{2AC}{g \cos \theta}} = \sqrt{\frac{2AB}{g}},$$

which is independent of θ.

The same reasoning will apply, if the highest point of the circle were taken instead of the lowest point.

135. A case of constrained motion was noticed in the description of Atwood's machine (Arts. 111, 112): the following are of a somewhat similar nature.

Let the body A draw the bodies B and C up the planes whose inclinations are ι, ι', by means of two inextensible strings.

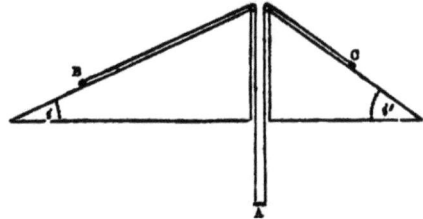

Then whatever space A descends through, B and C pass each of them through an equal space in the same time, therefore the motion of each of the bodies is the same.

Let T be the tension of the string connecting A and B, and T' that of the string connecting A and C: also let W, w, w', be the weights of A, B, C: then the force causing A to move downwards is $W - T - T'$; and the forces causing B and C to move up the inclined planes are respectively $T - w \sin \iota$, $T' - w' \sin \iota'$.

But on the body A the force W, on B the force w, and on C the force w', produces an acceleration g; therefore the accelerations on A, B, C are respectively

$$\frac{W - T - T'}{W} g, \quad \frac{T - w \sin \iota}{w} g, \quad \frac{T' - w' \sin \iota'}{w'} g :$$

all these three are equal, therefore each of them

$$= \frac{W - w \sin \iota - w' \sin \iota'}{W + w + w'} g,$$

which is constant. The motion of each body then is that in Arts. 38—41.

T and T' are easily obtained by equating the accelerations on B and C to the expression last found.

136. Suppose there to be only one string, and A to be suspended by a pulley: then the tension throughout is the same, T; and the accelerations on A, B, C are respectively

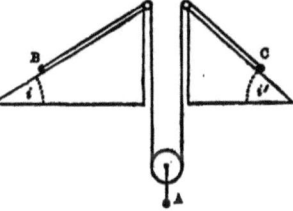

$$\frac{W - 2T}{W} g, \quad \frac{T - w \sin \iota}{w} g, \quad \frac{T - w' \sin \iota'}{w'} g :$$

and we have to consider the effect of the particular kind of constraint in this case.

If B were to move over any space, and C were immoveable, A would move over half that space, by the property of the simple moveable pulley; and so if C were to move, and B were fixed. Therefore A moves over half the sum of the spaces passed over by B and C, whatever these may be; therefore the acceleration on $A =$ half the sum of the accelerations on B and C;

i.e. $\quad \dfrac{W - 2T}{W} g = \tfrac{1}{2} \left(\dfrac{T - w \sin \iota}{w} g + \dfrac{T - w' \sin \iota'}{w'} g \right).$

This equation will give T, and then the accelerations on A, B, C will be determined.

In both these cases the pressures on the planes can be found, as in Art. 131, to be $w \cos \iota$, $w' \cos \iota'$.

Δ. 137. The general case of motion on a smooth plane curve is determined in the following manner :—

Take a pair of rectangular axes in the plane of the curve, and let α_x, α_y, be the accelerations on the motion in directions of x and y, arising from the external forces, and ξ the acceleration due to the force of constraint, which is in the direction of the normal at any point: then if m be the mass of the particle, $m\alpha_x$, $m\alpha_y$, are the forces acting on it, and $m\xi$ is the force of constraint (Art. 107); and we have

$$\left. \begin{aligned} \frac{d^2x}{dt^2} &= \alpha_x - \xi \frac{dy}{ds} \\ \frac{d^2y}{dt^2} &= \alpha_y + \xi \frac{dx}{ds} \end{aligned} \right\},$$

these, together with the equation to the curve, determine the motion.

We obtain immediately

$$2 \frac{dx}{dt} \frac{d^2x}{dt^2} + 2 \frac{dy}{dt} \frac{d^2y}{dt^2} = 2\alpha_x \frac{dx}{dt} + 2\alpha_y \frac{dy}{dt};$$

$$\therefore \left(\frac{dx}{dt}\right)^2 + \left(\frac{dy}{dt}\right)^2 = 2 \int (\alpha_x dx + \alpha_y dy):$$

this gives the velocity at any point.

We might have used tangential and normal resolutions, and then

$$\left. \begin{aligned} \frac{d^2 s}{dt^2} &= \alpha_x \frac{dx}{ds} + \alpha_y \frac{dy}{ds} \\ \frac{v^2}{\rho} &= \xi - \alpha_x \frac{dy}{ds} + \alpha_y \frac{dx}{ds} \end{aligned} \right\rangle,$$

which would give the same result more easily.

From the second of these, ξ, and therefore the force of constraint $m\xi$, is determined.

Δ. 138. If the only force acting be the weight of the particle, then taking the axis of x vertically downwards, the above equations become

$$\left. \begin{aligned} \frac{d^2 x}{dt^2} &= g - \xi \frac{dy}{ds} \\ \frac{d^2 y}{dt^2} &= \xi \frac{dx}{ds} \end{aligned} \right\rangle,$$

or

$$\left. \begin{aligned} \frac{d^2 s}{dt^2} &= g \frac{dx}{ds} \\ \frac{v^2}{\rho} &= \xi - g \frac{dy}{ds} \end{aligned} \right\rangle.$$

whence $\left(\dfrac{ds}{dt}\right)^2 = C + 2gx.$

If the initial value of x be a, and the initial velocity be v', this becomes

$$v^2 - v'^2 = 2g(x - a),$$

or the change of velocity is only due to the vertical space descended, as before (Art. 133).

Δ. 139. The pressure of the particle on the curve is $-m\xi$, the positive direction of ξ being towards the center of curvature.

When the particle is merely *on* the curve, since the reaction can never be in the direction from the particle to the curve, whenever ξ takes the value zero, the particle will leave the curve. If, however, the reaction be capable of being exerted in any direction, as in the case of a particle in a tube, there will be no such limitation.

140. To determine the motion of a heavy particle on a cycloid whose axis is vertical and vertex downwards.

Let P be the position of the particle at any time, A the vertex of the cycloid, RPT the generating circle, whose diameter RT is vertical and $= 2a$.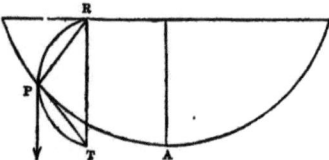

Then PT is a tangent to the cycloid (Appendix, Art. 2).

The acceleration on the particle in the direction of its motion

$$= g \cos PTR = g \frac{PT}{RT} = \frac{g}{2} \frac{AP}{RT} \text{ (App. Art. 3).}$$

$$= \frac{g}{4a} AP:$$

this varies as the distance from A.

The other part of the force and the constraint are only concerned with changing the direction of the motion, i. e. keeping the particle on the curve.

This kind of motion has been investigated in Arts. 51—54, and in Newton, § ij.

The particle will oscillate between two points equally distant from A, the time of a complete oscillation being $\dfrac{2\pi}{\sqrt{\dfrac{g}{4a}}}$.

The velocity at any point is determined from the considerations in Art. 133.

Δ. 141.· This may be easily got from the equations to the cycloid

$$x = a\,(1 - \cos\theta), \quad y = a\,(\theta + \sin\theta)\,; \quad \text{(App. Art. 5),}$$

where the axis of x is measured vertically upwards.

Then $\dfrac{d^2s}{dt^2} = -g\dfrac{dx}{ds}$ is the equation of motion.

And $\dfrac{dx}{d\theta} = a\sin\theta\,; \qquad \dfrac{ds}{d\theta} = 2a\cos\dfrac{\theta}{2}\,;$

$$\therefore \frac{dx}{ds} = \sin\frac{\theta}{2}\,;$$

$$\therefore \frac{d^2s}{dt^2} = -g\sin\frac{\theta}{2} = -g\,\frac{s}{4a}.$$

Therefore from Arts. 51—54, the motion is oscillatory and the time of a complete oscillation is $\dfrac{2\pi}{\sqrt{\dfrac{g}{4a}}}$.

142. It must be observed that in this case of motion the time of one oscillation is independent of the initial distance, or the oscillations in a cycloid are isochronous.

143. By means of two vertical semi-cycloidal cheeks connected so as to form a cusp, a particle suspended by a string can be made to oscillate in a cycloid, as indicated in App. Art. 4: the string will manifestly be always stretched. This forms a "simple pendulum." The length of this string is $4a = l$ say, and therefore the time of a complete oscillation $= 2\pi\sqrt{\dfrac{l}{g}}$.

In pendulums the time of an oscillation is generally taken to be the time from rest to rest, and therefore it $= \pi\sqrt{\dfrac{l}{g}}$.

This formula is made great use of for finding the value of g: for the length l of a seconds' pendulum can be determined with great accuracy[*], and then we have $1 = \pi\sqrt{\dfrac{l}{g}}$, whence $g = \pi^2 l$:

[*] The manner in which this is ascertained will be found in Griffin's *Dynamics of a Rigid Body.*

the units in which g is expressed are seconds, and whatever unit of length is assumed in l.

The length of a seconds pendulum = 39·1392 inches, very nearly, i. e. 3·2616 feet; and putting $\pi = 3·1416$, we have

$$g = 32·19 \text{ feet per second, nearly.}$$

144. To determine the motion of a heavy particle in a vertical circle.

If the motion is very small, it will consist of small oscillations about the lowest point, which can be deduced from the case of the cycloid, the time of one of these complete oscillations being $2\pi \sqrt{\dfrac{l}{g}}$, where l is the radius of the circle.

In other cases we must proceed as follows:

Let C be the initial position of the particle, P its position at any time, A the lowest point of the circle, O its center, $a =$ its radius, v, $v' =$ the velocities at P, C respectively, angle $AOP = \theta$, $AOC = a$; and CM, PN horizontal lines.

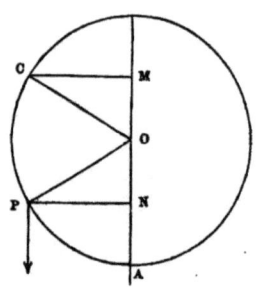

Then the change of velocity from C to P is due to the vertical space descended (Art. 133);

$$\therefore \ v^2 - v'^2 = 2g \cdot MN = 2ga \, (\cos \theta - \cos a).$$

Let ξ be the acceleration due to the force of constraint in the normal, considered positive if towards O.

Then $\dfrac{v^2}{a} =$ acceleration in $PO = \xi - g \cos \theta$ (NEWTON, § ij);

$$\therefore \ \xi = g \cos \theta + \frac{v^2}{a}$$

$$= g \cos \theta + 2g \, (\cos \theta - \cos a) + \frac{v'^2}{a}$$

$$= g \, (3 \cos \theta - 2 \cos a) + \frac{v'^2}{a};$$

L.

M

therefore if R be the force of constraint, and W the weight of the particle,

$$\frac{R}{W} = \frac{\xi}{g} \ (\text{Art. } 105 \ (4)) ;$$

$$\therefore \ R = W \left(3 \cos \theta - 2 \cos \alpha + \frac{v'^2}{ga} \right).$$

If the particle be on the outside of the circle, R must never be positive; if on the inside, or if suspended from O by a string, R must never be negative; but if the particle be moving in a circular tube or groove, or be connected with O by a rigid rod, R may be either positive or negative.

145.   If the particle be initially at rest, $v' = 0$; and then

$$\left. \begin{array}{l} v^2 = 2ga \ (\cos \theta - \cos \alpha) \\ R = W \ (3 \cos \theta - 2 \cos \alpha) \end{array} \right\} ;$$

whence $\cos \theta > \cos \alpha$, or θ lies between $+ \alpha$ and $- \alpha$; therefore the motion is oscillatory between the points for which $\theta = + \alpha$ and $- \alpha$.

The greatest value of R in any case is when $\cos \theta$ is greatest, i.e. when $\theta = 0$, or at the lowest point.

If the particle start from rest at the highest point, $\alpha = \pi$, and the greatest value of R is $5W$.

146.   If the particle be suspended by a string, making complete revolutions, and if the velocity at the highest point be just sufficient to keep the string stretched,

then ξ, which $= g \cos \theta + \dfrac{v^2}{a}$, must $= 0$, when $\theta = \pi$, $v = v'$;

$$\therefore \ v'^2 = ga.$$

And we have $R = W \ (3 \cos \theta - 2 \cos \alpha + 1)$

$$= 3W \ (1 + \cos \theta), \text{ for } \alpha = \pi.$$

The greatest value of this is $6W$: i.e. the string must be able to bear six times the weight of the particle without breaking, in order that this motion may continue.

147. The motion of Art. 145 will not apply to a particle suspended by a string unless R is always positive: the least value of R corresponds to the least value of $\cos \theta$, i.e. when $\theta = \alpha$, and R then becomes $W \cos \alpha$. If this is positive, α must not exceed $\frac{\pi}{2}$: therefore oscillatory motion of a particle suspended by a string is not possible unless the extent of oscillation be not greater than a semicircle.

Δ. 148. All this might have been obtained by means of the equations in Arts. 34 or 35; which, remembering that in a circle r is constant and $= a$, and $s = a\theta$, become

$$\left. \begin{array}{l} a \left(\dfrac{d\theta}{dt} \right)^2 = \xi - g \cos \theta \\[2mm] a \dfrac{d^2\theta}{dt^2} = -g \sin \theta \end{array} \right\} .$$

If θ be so small that its cube and higher powers may be neglected, the second equation becomes

$$\frac{d^2\theta}{dt^2} = -\frac{g}{a}\theta;$$

whence, by Arts. 51—54, the motion will be oscillatory, and the time of a complete oscillation will be $2\pi \sqrt{\dfrac{a}{g}}$; therefore a pendulum oscillating in a circle may be considered as one oscillating in a cycloid, when the arc of vibration is so small that its cube and higher powers may be neglected.

In other cases $\qquad \dfrac{d^2\theta}{dt^2} = -\dfrac{g}{a} \sin \theta;$

$$\therefore \ 2 \frac{d\theta}{dt} \frac{d^2\theta}{dt^2} = -2\frac{g}{a} \sin \theta \frac{d\theta}{dt};$$

$$\therefore \ \left(\frac{d\theta}{dt} \right)^2 = 2\frac{g}{a} (\cos \theta - \cos \alpha);$$

whence $\qquad \xi = g \cos \theta + a \left(\dfrac{d\theta}{dt} \right)^2$

$$= g \, (3 \cos \theta - 2 \cos \alpha):$$

the particle having been supposed to start from rest at a point for which $\theta = a$.

Δ. 149. To determine the motion of a heavy particle hanging by an elastic string, it having been vertically displaced from its position of rest.

Since the only forces acting are the weight of the particle and the tension of the string, the directions of which are both vertical, the motion is rectilinear.

Let W be the weight of the particle, a the natural length of the string: then in the position of equilibrium the length of the string $= a \left(1 + \dfrac{W}{E} \right)$, E being the weight which will stretch the string to twice its natural length.

Let $a \left(1 + \dfrac{W}{E} \right) + x$ be the length of the string at any time t, and T its tension.

Then $\qquad a \left(1 + \dfrac{W}{E} \right) + x = a \left(1 + \dfrac{T}{E} \right),$

$$\text{whence } \quad T = W + E . \frac{x}{a} .$$

The downward force on the particle is $W - T$, or $- E . \dfrac{x}{a}$;

therefore the acceleration downwards is $- \dfrac{E}{W} . \dfrac{x}{a} . g$;

$$\therefore \overline{\frac{d}{dt}}\Big|^2 . \left\{ a \left(1 + \frac{W}{E} \right) + x \right\}, \text{ or } \frac{d^2 x}{dt^2} = - \frac{E}{W} . \frac{x}{a} g,$$

which varies as x.

The motion then is that investigated in Art. 51, and therefore the particle makes oscillations about its position of statical equilibrium, the time of each being $\dfrac{2\pi}{\sqrt{\dfrac{E}{W} . \dfrac{g}{a}}}$.

E. g. If the natural length of the string be 4 yards, and if it be stretched $\frac{1}{4}$ inch by a weight of 1 lb.; the weight being slightly depressed, to find the time of an oscillation.

Take 1 foot, 1 second, and 1 lb. for the units of length, time, and force.

Then $a = 12$, $W = 1$, $g = 32\cdot2$; and to find E we have

$$1 : E :: \tfrac{1}{4} \text{ inch} : 4 \text{ yards}; \quad \therefore E = 576.$$

And the time of a complete oscillation

$$= 2\pi \div \sqrt{576 \times \frac{32\cdot2}{12}} \text{ seconds}$$

$$= \tfrac{1}{2}\pi \sqrt{\frac{1}{3 \times 32\cdot2}} = \cdot16 \text{ seconds, nearly.}$$

Δ. 150. To determine the motion of a particle suspended by an inelastic string to a point, and revolving in space with an uniform angular velocity about a vertical line through that point.

Let O be the fixed point, P the position of the particle at time t, OA the vertical line, PN perpendicular to OA, NM parallel to the initial position of PN,

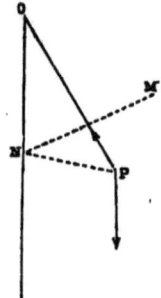

$$PON = \phi, \quad OP = a, \quad ON = z;$$

$PN = r$, $MNP = \theta$, the polar co-ordinates of P in the plane perpendicular to OA.

Then $r = a \sin\phi$, $z = a \cos\phi$, $\theta = \omega t$ (ω being the angular velocity about OA).

The forces acting on P are its weight downwards, i.e. in the direction of z, and the tension of the string in the direction PO; which produce accelerations g and ξ say: therefore the acceleration in z is $g - \xi \cos\phi$, that in r is $-\xi \sin\phi$, and that at right angles to r and z is 0;

$$\left. \begin{aligned}
\therefore \frac{d^2r}{dt^2} - r\left(\frac{d\theta}{dt}\right)^2 &= -\xi \sin\phi, \\
\frac{1}{r}\frac{d}{dt}\left(r^2\frac{d\theta}{dt}\right) &= 0, \\
\frac{d^2z}{dt^2} &= g - \xi \cos\phi.
\end{aligned} \right\} \quad \text{(Arts. 32, 33).}$$

Since $\dfrac{d\theta}{dt} = \omega$ a constant, the second equation shews that r is constant; and therefore $\sin \phi$, which $= \dfrac{r}{a}$, is constant, and consequently z, which $= a \cos \phi$, is constant.

Therefore from the first equation,

$$\omega^2 r = \xi \sin \phi,$$

$$\text{or } \xi = \omega^2 a;$$

and from the third,

$$g - \xi \cos \phi = 0,$$

$$\text{or } \cos \phi = \frac{g}{\omega^2 a}.$$

From these it appears that the particle describes a circle whose center is N, a fixed point; and that the string is inclined to the vertical line OA at the same angle $\left(\cos^{-1} \dfrac{g}{\omega^2 a} \right)$ throughout the motion.

This motion is similar to that of the 'governor' of a steam-engine.

CHAPTER IX.

151. THE forces we have hitherto considered have required a finite time in which to act in order that they might generate an appreciable velocity in a particle, but cases occur in which forces are brought into action for an inappreciably small time and yet a finite velocity is generated: such forces are called impulses. Of course they will be measured in an analogous way to that in which all other forces are measured, and therefore their measures will be proportional to the accelerations they would produce, i.e. to the velocities they would generate in an unit of time, supposing them to be constantly acting for that unit. But these would be infinitely great, therefore we must seek for some other measure of an impulse. Now with an uniform acceleration, we have $v = at$ (Art. 21); therefore if t be the same for a set of accelerations, v will vary as a, and therefore the measure of an impulse will vary as the velocity it generates *in any assigned time*. We shall assume that the inappreciably small times for which impulses act are appreciably equal; then the measure of an impulse will vary as the velocity it *actually* generates. This is as long as the same quantity of matter is acted on: and when different particles are acted on and the same velocity is generated, the measure of an impulse will of course vary as the measure of the quantity of matter, as in Art. 106. Then if with the unit of impulse acting on a particle of mass M' a velocity v' is generated, and with the impulse R acting on the mass M a velocity v is generated, we have

$$R : 1 :: Mv : M'v'.$$

As M' and v' are arbitrary, let them both $= 1$; this fixes the unit of impulse to be that which generates the unit of velocity when acting on the unit of mass, and then we have $R = Mv$: therefore the measure of an impulse is the *momentum* produced by it (Art. 109).

152. No confusion can be introduced by this modification, for the effects of finite forces can never appear as long as the effects of impulses are being considered; and after that the impulses have ceased to act, and we have only certain velocities affected by certain finite forces.

153. The mutual action at the surfaces of two smooth bodies in contact is normal to both surfaces, for otherwise it would have a tangential component which would make one body slip along the other. So also the mutual action between a particle and a smooth surface with which it is in contact, is normal to the surface.

In the collision of smooth balls (treated as particles) we shall have to consider them as elastic or inelastic; moreover the directions of their motions may be coincident with the line in which the impulse takes place or not.

154. If a ball of ivory be thrown against a plane surface smeared slightly with some discolouring matter, it is found that the ball has, not a point, but a finite portion of its surface discoloured; its spherical form however remains as before: this shews that it has been compressed and that its original form has been regained. This property is called elasticity, and it exists more or less in all bodies with which we are acquainted. The force called into action to restore the form is evidently that which causes the rebound in such an experiment as the above, so that a perfectly inelastic body (if we could take such an one) would not separate from anything after an impact with it.

155. To determine the effect of the collision of two inelastic balls moving with given velocities in the line of impact. This is a case of direct impact.

Let M, M' be the masses of the balls A and B respectively; V, V' their velocities, taking account of algebraic signs for direction;

B the impulse between them, measured by the momentum generated (Art. 151), which must be the same for each, and in opposite directions, by the Third Law of Motion (Art. 110); so that if A impinges on B, the impulse R increases B's motion and diminishes A's. As the balls are inelastic, they do not separate after the impact, therefore they move with a common velocity; let this be v.

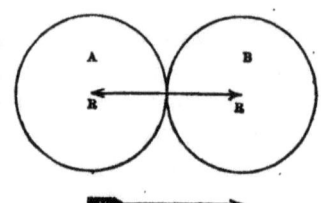

Before the impact the momenta of A and B are respectively

$$MV, \quad M'V' ;$$

therefore after the impact, the momentum of $A = MV - R$, and that of $B = M'V' + R$;

$$\left. \begin{array}{l} \therefore \text{ the velocity of } A = V - \dfrac{R}{M} \\[2mm] \text{and the velocity of } B = V' + \dfrac{R}{M'} \end{array} \right\} \text{(Art. 109)};$$

$$\therefore v = V - \frac{R}{M} = V' + \frac{R}{M'} ;$$

whence $\qquad R = \dfrac{MM'}{M + M'} (V - V')$,

and $\qquad v = V - \dfrac{M'}{M + M'} (V - V')$

$$= \frac{MV + M'V'}{M + M'} .$$

This gives the common velocity after impact.

156. From the equation $Mv + M'v = MV + M'V'$ we see that the momentum of the system before impact is equal to the momentum afterwards.

157. If the balls be elastic, we have to consider (1) the circumstances of their mutual compression, (2) the circumstances of their restitution of figure. We have then two impulses,

R for the compression, and R' for the restitution of figure, the whole impulse being $R + R'$, which increases B's motion and diminishes A's. During the compression the impulse R' has not been acting, and therefore the circumstances are the same as if the balls were inelastic; therefore R is the same in this case as in the former, and consequently $= \dfrac{MM'}{M + M'} (V - V')$.

Let v, v' be the velocities of A and B after impact; therefore their momenta after impact are $Mv, M'v'$;

$$\therefore \quad Mv = MV - (R + R'), \\ M'v' = M'V' + (R + R').$$

It is also supposed that R' bears to R a ratio depending only upon the nature of the substances that impinge, so that $R' = eR$, where e depends only upon the nature of the materials of which A and B are composed. e is called the modulus of elasticity, and lies between 0 and 1: if $e = 1$, the elasticity is said to be perfect, but we know of no such case in nature.

Then we have
$$v = V - (1 + e) \frac{R}{M} \\ v' = V' + (1 + e) \frac{R}{M'},$$

where $R = \dfrac{MM'}{M + M'} (V - V')$;

$$\therefore v = V - (1 + e) \frac{M'}{M + M'} (V - V') \\ v' = V' + (1 + e) \frac{M}{M + M'} (V - V'),$$

which equations determine the subsequent motion.

158. Also we have
$$v' - v = - (V - V') + (1 + e)(V - V') \\ = e(V - V'),$$

or the velocity of separation of the balls after impact : the velocity of approach before impact :: $e : 1$.

· · This is a property that can be tested by observation, and establishes the correctness of our hypothesis that $R' = eR$. For if we had started with the equations

$$\left. \begin{array}{l} Mv = MV - (R + R') \\ M'v' = M'V' + (R + R') \\ R = \dfrac{MM'}{M + M'}(V - V') \end{array} \right\}$$

and *assumed* that $v' - v = e(V - V')$, we should directly have obtained $R' = eR$.

159. We have also $Mv + M'v' = MV + M'V'$ in this case as well as in the preceding, so that no momentum is lost by the impact.

160. If x, x' be the distances of the centers of the balls from any fixed point in the line of impact at time t after the collision, we have

$$\left. \begin{array}{l} x = a + vt \\ x' = a' + v't \end{array} \right\},$$

a, a' being the initial values of x, x'.

And if $\bar{x}$ be the distance of the center of gravity of the two from the same point,

$$\bar{x} = \frac{Mx + M'x'}{M + M'}$$

$$= \frac{Ma + M'a' + (Mv + M'v')t}{M + M'}$$

$$= \frac{Ma + M'a'}{M + M'} + \frac{MV + M'V'}{M + M'} \cdot t;$$

therefore the velocity of the center of gravity of the two balls after impact is $\dfrac{MV + M'V'}{M + M'}$, the same as its velocity before impact.

161. If the impact be not direct, i. e. if the balls be initially moving in directions not coincident with the line of impulse, we must resolve their velocities into the directions of the line of impulse and perpendicular to it. The resolved parts in the direction of impulse will be affected by the impact after the manner of the preceding investigations: those perpendicular to that direction will not be affected at all, because the balls are smooth. Then the velocities of either ball in the direction perpendicular to the line of impulse before and after the impact are equal; and the equations of the preceding Articles will be true in this case, wherein V, V', v, v', represent the resolved parts of the velocities in the direction of impact.

162. In the collision of two perfectly elastic balls, the *vis viva* of the system after impact is the same as that before impact.

By the *vis viva* of the system is meant the sum of the *vires vivæ* of the balls. (See Art. 109.)

We have, using the notation of Art. 157,

$$v - v' = -e(V - V')$$
$$= -(V - V'),$$

because the elasticity is perfect;

$$\text{and } Mv + M'v' = MV + M'V'.$$
$$\text{Whence } M(v - V) = M'(V' - v'),$$
$$\text{and } v + V = V' + v';$$
$$\therefore M(v^2 - V^2) = M'(V'^2 - v'^2),$$
$$\text{or } Mv^2 + M'v'^2 = MV^2 + M'V'^2.$$

163. If the elasticity be imperfect, *vis viva* is lost by the collision.

$$\text{For } \left. \begin{array}{l} v - v' = -e(V - V') \\ Mv + M'v' = MV + M'V' \end{array} \right\};$$
$$\therefore M(v - V) = M'(V' - v'),$$
$$\text{and } v + V = v' + V' + (1 - e)(V - V');$$

$$\therefore\ M(v^2 - V^2) = M'(V'^2 - v'^2) + (1 - e)M'(V' - v')(V - V').$$

Also $\quad v' = V' + \dfrac{(1+e)M}{M+M'}(V - V')$,

or $\quad v' - V' = \dfrac{(1+e)M}{M+M'}(V - V')$;

$$\therefore\ M(v^2 - V^2) = M'(V'^2 - v'^2) - (1 - e)M' \cdot \dfrac{(1+e)M}{M+M'}(V - V')^2,$$

or $\quad Mv^2 + M'v'^2 = MV^2 + M'V'^2 - (1 - e^2)\dfrac{MM'}{M+M'}(V - V')^2$,

which is less than $MV^2 + M'V'^2$, $\because e < 1$.

164. An elastic ball strikes a smooth plane obliquely: to determine the motion.

If a plane be drawn through the initial direction of motion and the normal to the plane against which the ball impinges, there is no velocity and no impulse perpendicular to this plane, and therefore after impact the ball will still move in it. Let this plane be that in which the annexed figure is drawn, so that the plane against which the ball impinges is perpendicular to that of the paper.

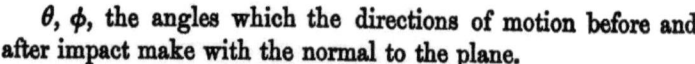

Let v, v' be the velocities of the ball before and after impact,

M its mass,

$(1 + e)R$ the impulse,

θ, ϕ, the angles which the directions of motion before and after impact make with the normal to the plane.

Then as the impulse does not affect the velocity resolved in the direction of the plane, we have

$$v \sin \theta = v' \sin \phi.$$

For the motion perpendicular to the plane, we have

$$v' \cos \phi = v \cos \theta - (1 + e)\frac{R}{M}.$$

R is determined by the supposition of inelasticity, i. e. that an inelastic body would after the impact have no velocity perpendicular to the plane;

$$\therefore \; 0 = v \cos \theta - \frac{R}{M}.$$

And then we immediately get

$$v' \cos \phi = - ev \cos \theta.$$

Combining these results we get

$$\left. \begin{array}{l} \cot \phi = - e \cot \theta \\ v' = v \sqrt{\sin^2\theta + e^2 \cos^2\theta} \end{array} \right\}.$$

These determine the direction of motion and the velocity after impact. It appears from them that the ball rebounds on the opposite side of the normal to that on which it impinges, the direction of its motion making a greater *acute* angle with it after the impact than before; its velocity is diminished by the impact. In the case of perfect elasticity, the velocities before and after impact are equal, and in directions equally inclined to the normal on opposite sides of it.

APPENDIX.

1. IF a circle roll on a straight line, any point in its circumference will trace out a cycloid.

It is evident that the form of the curve will be such as that

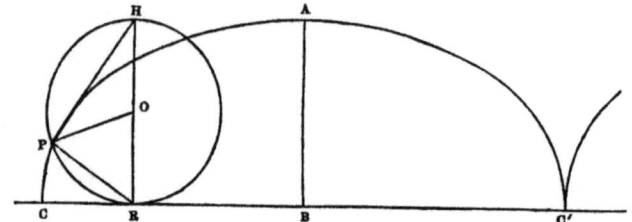

in the figure, P being the point in the generating circle which traces it, and CC' the line on which the circle rolls. The curve may be continued to an unlimited extent, as indicated in the figure, where the beginning of the portion beyond C' is shewn; but we shall only consider the one portion CAC', with which all the others will be identical.

If AB bisect CC' at right angles, the curve will be symmetrical with respect to AB, which is called the axis of the cycloid. The point A is called the vertex and C, C' are cusps.

2. In the generating circle, if P be joined with the extremities of the diameter ROH, which passes through the point of contact R of the circle with the straight line CC', the line PH will be perpendicular to PR. And at the instant of time when the circle is in the position HPR, since it *rolls* along CBC' the point R is at rest, and therefore P is moving *at that*

instant as if describing a circle about R; therefore the motion of P is for the instant perpendicular to PR, and therefore is in the direction PH. Therefore PH is a tangent to the cycloid.

3. The arc of a cycloid measured from the vertex to any point is equal to twice the length of the portion of the tangent at that point intercepted by the generating circle passing through that point. $(AP = 2 \cdot PH)$.

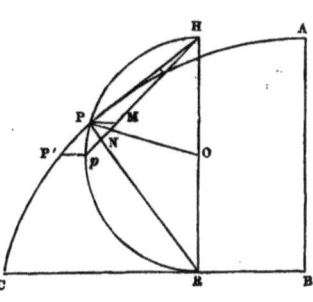

Take a point P' very near to P. Draw $P'p$ parallel to CB and join Hp. Then ultimately Hp is parallel to the tangent at P', and HP is the tangent at P; therefore if PM be drawn parallel to $P'p$, the figure $PMpP'$ is ultimately a parallelogram*, and $pM = PP'$. Also ultimately pH is perpendicular to PR, i. e. the angles PNp, PNM are ultimately right angles.

And the chord PR of the circle makes equal angles with the tangents at its extremities, therefore the angles pPR, CRP are ultimately equal; i. e. pPN, NPM are ultimately equal.

Therefore ultimately the triangles pPN, MPN have two angles equal each to each, and the side PN common; therefore ultimately $pN = NM$, or $pM = 2 \cdot pN$,

And ultimately $HN = HP$; therefore ultimately

$$PP' = 2 \cdot pN = 2 \, (Hp - HP),$$

i. e. the increment of the arc AP is twice the corresponding increment of the chord HP.

This arc and chord begin simultaneously from zero; therefore the arc $AP =$ twice the chord HP.

4. If two equal cycloids be placed with their axes parallel and a cusp of the one coincident with the vertex of the other, their concavities being turned towards the same parts; and if a

---

* The chords PP', Pp (which are ultimately coincident with the arcs PP', Pp) have not been drawn, to avoid complicating the figure.

tangent drawn at any point of the one within the concavity of the other be produced to meet it, it will be a normal to it, and will be equal in length to the arc of the first cycloid from the vertex to the point of contact.

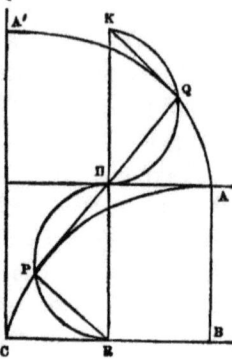

Take the generating circle in the position HPR: then PH is a tangent to the cycloid AC.

Produce RH to K, make $KH = RH$, and describe the semicircle KQH, which will $= RPH$. Produce PH to meet the semicircle KQH in Q, and join QK.

Then the angles PHR, KHQ are equal: therefore, since the circles are equal,

$$\text{arc } HQ = \text{arc } PH$$
$$= \text{arc } HPR - \text{arc } PR$$
$$= BC - RC, \text{ by the mode of generation of the cycloid,}$$
$$= AH.$$

Therefore Q is in the cycloid $A'A$: and HQK is its generating circle; therefore KQ is the tangent at Q, and consequently HQ is the normal.

Also as $PH = HQ$,

$$PQ = 2PH = \text{arc } AP.$$

From this it is evident that if a string fastened at C equal in length to CA be unwrapped from the cycloid CA, its extremity will trace out an equal cycloid in the position AA'.

Δ. 5. This may be investigated by means of the differential calculus. Take the vertex of the cycloid for origin, and its axis for the axis of x; and for any point $P(x, y)$ let the angle $POH = \theta$, HPR being the generating circle. Let the radius of this circle be a,

L.

O

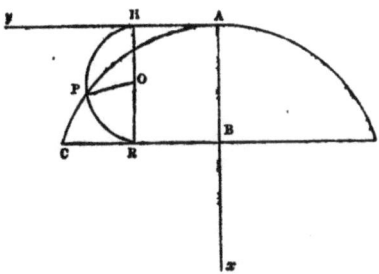

then $\quad x = HO + PO \cos POR = a - a \cos \theta,$

$\qquad y = BR + PO \sin POR$

$\qquad\quad = \text{arc } HP + PO \sin POR$

$\qquad\quad = a\theta + a \sin \theta \, ;$

$\therefore \; \left. \begin{aligned} x &= a\,(1 - \cos \theta) \\ y &= a\,(\theta + \sin \theta) \end{aligned} \right\} \quad (\alpha)\,;$

$\therefore \; \text{versin } \theta = \dfrac{x}{a},$

and $\dfrac{y}{a} = \theta + \sin \theta$

$\qquad\qquad = \text{versin}^{-1} \dfrac{x}{a} + \sqrt{1 - \left(\dfrac{a - x}{a}\right)^2},$

or $\quad y = a\, \text{versin}^{-1} \dfrac{x}{a} + \sqrt{2ax - x^2}.$

This is the equation to the cycloid, but the pair of equations (α) will perhaps be found more convenient.

We also have $\quad \dfrac{dx}{d\theta} = a \sin \theta,$

$\qquad\qquad\quad \dfrac{dy}{d\theta} = a\,(1 + \cos \theta)\,;$

$$\therefore \frac{ds}{d\theta} = + a \sqrt{\sin^2 \theta + (1 + \cos \theta)^2} *$$

$$= 2a \cos \frac{\theta}{2};$$

$\therefore s = 4a \sin \frac{\theta}{2}$, no constant being added, because at the point A (for which $\theta = 0$) $s = 0$.

But $2a \sin \frac{1}{2} POH = $ chord PH; therefore the arc of a cycloid measured from the vertex $= 2 \times$ chord of the generating circle touching the cycloid.

If ϕ be the inclination of the tangent at P to that at A, $\phi = PRH$ in the figure of Art. 4, and therefore $s = 4a \sin \phi$, which is the intrinsic equation to the cycloid.

Δ. 6. To find the involute of a cycloid produced by unwrapping a string from it whose length $=$ the semi-cycloid, the extremity of the string being initially at the vertex.

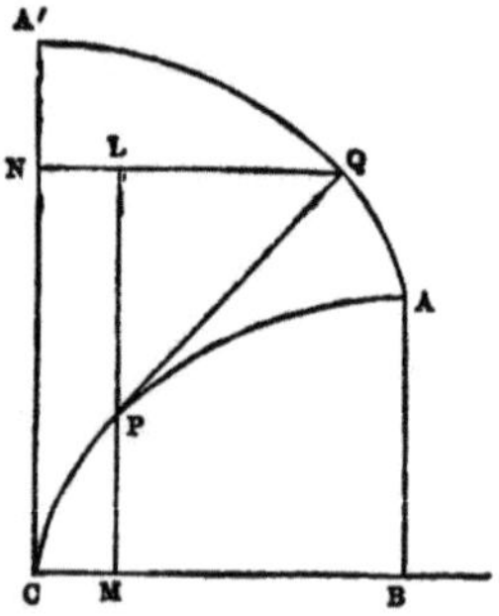

If $A'C$ be perpendicular to CB we shall have

$A'C = $ arc $AC = 2 \times$ chord of generating circle touching the cycloid at C

$= 4a;$

and $PQ = $ arc $AP = 4a \sin \frac{\theta}{2}.$

And referring to the figure of Art. 1,

angle $LPQ = PHR = \frac{1}{2}(\pi - \theta);$

$$\therefore QL = PQ \sin LPQ = PQ \cos \frac{\theta}{2} = 2a \sin \theta.$$

Also $CM = CB - BM = \pi a - a (\theta + \sin \theta)$

by the second of equations (a);

$$\therefore QN = QL + CM = a (\pi - \theta + \sin \theta).$$

Also $CN = PM + PQ \cos LPQ$

$$= AB - x + PQ \sin \frac{\theta}{2}$$

$$= 2a - a (1 - \cos \theta) + 4a \sin^2 \frac{\theta}{2}$$

$$= a (3 - \cos \theta);$$

* The positive sign is taken, because s increases with θ.

$$\therefore \ A'N = A'C - CN$$

$$= a\,(1 + \cos\theta).$$

These values of AN, QN can be got from those of x and y in equations (a) by writing $\pi - \theta$ instead of θ, and therefore we see that the involute is an equal cycloid whose vertex is A' and axis $A'C$.

By means of the intrinsic equation this may very easily be obtained: for let A' be the origin of measurement for the curve $A'Q$,

then $\dfrac{ds'}{d\phi'}$ = radius of curvature at $Q = PQ$ evidently, $= s$,

and $QPL = \phi' = \dfrac{\pi}{2} - \phi$;

$$\therefore \ \frac{ds'}{d\phi'} = 4a \cos \phi';$$

whence $s' = 4a \sin \phi'$,

which represents an equal cycloid.

PROBLEMS.

*** The usual notation has been adopted in these Problems, excepting where it differs from that in the preceding chapters; it is therefore thought unnecessary to explain the meaning of the symbols in every case.

CHAPTERS I, II.

1. THE measures of an acceleration and a velocity when referred respectively to $(a + b)$ ft., $(m + n)''$, and $(a - b)$ ft., $(m - n)''$ as units, are in the inverse ratio of their measures when referred to $(a - b)$ ft., $(m - n)''$, and $(a + b)$ ft., $(m + n)''$; their measures when referred to a ft., m'', and b ft., n'', are as $ma : nb$. Shew that $\dfrac{n}{m} = \sqrt{1 - \dfrac{b^4}{a^4}}$.

Let a, v, be their measures when referred to 1 ft., 1''.

Then, by Arts. 6, 27,

$$\frac{(m + n)^2}{a + b} a : \frac{m - n}{a - b} v :: \frac{m + n}{a + b} v : \frac{(m - n)^2}{a - b} a \ldots\ldots\ldots(1),$$
$$\frac{m^2}{a} a : \frac{n}{b} v :: ma : nb \ldots\ldots\ldots\ldots\ldots\ldots(2).$$

From (1), $(m^2 - n^2) a^2 = v^2$,

from (2), $\dfrac{a}{b} v = \dfrac{mb}{a} a$,

whence $(m^2 - n^2) \dfrac{a^2}{b^2} = \dfrac{m^2 b^2}{a^2}$;

$\therefore \dfrac{n}{m} = \sqrt{1 - \dfrac{b^4}{a^4}}$.

2. Two candles, which will burn for 4 and 6 hours respectively, are placed in candlesticks 1 foot high and 1 foot apart, and are lighted simultaneously. The shadow of the shorter is received on the table on which they stand: that of the longer on a wall 10 feet distant from it, and perpendicular to the plane of the candles. Each candle is originally 1 foot long: find the velocity of the extremity of the shadow of the longer. Find also the mean velocity of the extremity of the shadow of the shorter during the last hour in which it is burning.

Let ABC, DEF represent the candles at any time, and GH the wall.

Then the motion of the extremity of the shadow on the wall consists of two parts, (1) that due to the burning of A, D being stationary; (2) that due to the burning of D, A being stationary.

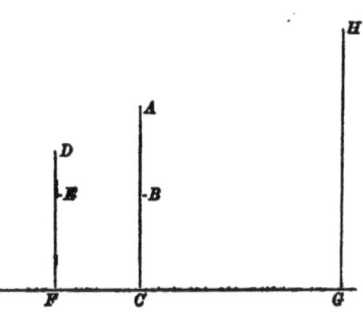

(1) If A passes over a space a in any time, the extremity of the shadow moves downward over $\dfrac{GF}{CF} a$ in the same time.

(2) If D passes over a' in any time, the shadow moves upward over $\dfrac{GC}{CF} a'$.

If then the time assumed in the above be the unit of time, the velocity of the extremity of the shadow downwards is

$$\frac{GF}{CF} a - \frac{GC}{CF} a', \text{ or } \frac{1}{CF}(a.GF - a'.GC),$$

where a, a' represent the velocities of A, D.

Take 1 foot and 1 hour for units.

Then $CF = 1$, $GC = 10$, $a = \frac{1}{6}$, $a' = \frac{1}{4}$;

therefore the velocity required $= \frac{1}{6}.11 - \frac{1}{4}.10 = -\frac{2}{3}$,

or 8 inches per hour upwards.

Second part.

Join AD and produce it to K.

At the beginning of the last hour $FD = 1\frac{1}{4}$, $CA = 1\frac{1}{2}$, $FE = CB = CF = 1$.

And at time t (expressed in hours) after this

$$FD = 1\frac{1}{4} - \frac{1}{4}t, \quad AC = 1\frac{1}{2} - \frac{1}{8}t;$$

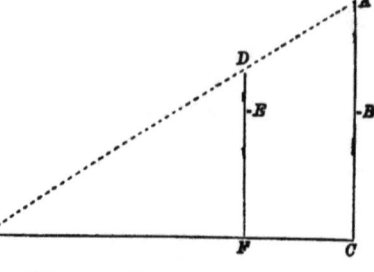

$$\therefore CK = AC \cdot \frac{CF}{AC - FD} = \frac{24}{3+t} - 2.$$

To find the velocity of K take a small time τ immediately subsequent to t: then the space passed over is

$$\frac{24}{3+t+\tau} - \frac{24}{3+t}, \text{ which} = -\frac{24\tau}{(t+3)(t+3+\tau)};$$

therefore (by Art. 14), the velocity $= -\dfrac{24}{(t+3)(t+3+\tau)}$,

when τ is indefinitely diminished,

$$\text{and therefore} = -\frac{24}{(t+3)^2}.$$

As t changes from 0 to 1, the greatest and least values of this will be $-\dfrac{8}{3}$, $-\dfrac{3}{2}$: and the mean of these is $-2\frac{1}{12}$;

therefore the mean velocity is 25 inches per hour towards F.

If the mean velocity be considered to be the velocity with which the point would describe *uniformly* the space which it does describe, in the same time, we have

at the beginning of the last hour $CK = 6$,

and at the end $CK = 4$;

therefore the space passed over by K is 2 feet, i.e. its mean velocity is 2 feet per hour.

Δ. 3. If a point be moving in a plane, the normal acceleration being n times the tangential, and the velocity at a point, the distance of which from some fixed point, measured along the curve, is s, varying as $\epsilon^{\frac{1}{n}\tan^{-1}\frac{s}{c}}$; when c is a constant: shew that the path of the moving point is a catenary.

We have $\dfrac{v^2}{\rho} = n\dfrac{d^2s}{dt^2}$, and $\dfrac{ds}{dt} = \lambda\epsilon^{\frac{1}{n}\tan^{-1}\frac{s}{c}}$;

therefore if ϕ be the angle in the intrinsic equation

$$\frac{d\phi}{ds}\left(\frac{ds}{dt}\right)^2, \text{ or } \frac{d\phi}{dt}\cdot\frac{ds}{dt} = n\frac{d^2s}{dt^2}$$

$$= n\,.\,\lambda\epsilon^{\frac{1}{n}\tan^{-1}\frac{s}{c}}\cdot\frac{1}{n}\cdot\frac{c}{s^2+c^2}\cdot\frac{ds}{dt};$$

$$\therefore \frac{d\phi}{dt} = \frac{c}{s^2+c^2}\frac{ds}{dt},$$

$$\text{or } \phi+\beta = \tan^{-1}\frac{s}{c}.$$

Suppose that the initial values of ϕ and s are both 0, then $s = c\tan\phi$; therefore the path is a catenary.

4. A person travelling eastward at the rate of 4 miles an hour, observes that the wind seems to blow from the north; on doubling his speed, the wind seems to blow from the north-east. Determine the direction and the velocity of the wind.

$$[4\sqrt{2}\text{ miles per hour, from N.W.}]$$

5. If a_1, a_2, be the measures of an acceleration referred to $(m+n)''$, a ft., and $(m-n)''$, b ft., as units; then its measure when referred to $(2m)''$, c ft., is

$$\frac{(\sqrt{aa_1}+\sqrt{ba_2})^2}{c}.$$

6. If the acceleration of gravity (32 feet per second) be the unit of acceleration, and the rate of 10 miles per hour be the unit of velocity, what must be the units of space and time?

$$\left[6\text{ ft. }8\tfrac{2}{3}\text{ in.}; \frac{11}{24}\text{ sec.}\right]$$

Δ. 7. If the axes of x and y turn about the origin with the same uniform angular velocity ω, find expressions for the accelerations parallel to them.

$$\left[\frac{d^2x}{dt^2} - \omega^2x - 2\omega\frac{dy}{dt}; \quad \frac{d^2y}{dt^2} - \omega^2y + 2\omega\frac{dx}{dt}.\right]$$

CHAPTER III.

8. If a straight line be drawn in a given direction from the initial position of a point whose motion is affected by a constant acceleration in another given direction: find the condition that the point may cross the line at right angles, and the distance from its initial position at which it will do so.

Let the straight line be inclined at an angle $\frac{\pi}{2} + \beta$ to the direction of the constant acceleration a, and let the initial direction of motion be inclined at the angle θ to this line, which take for the axis of x.

Then the acceleration in x is $-a \sin \beta$,

and that in y is $-a \cos \beta$.

And we have
$$\left. \begin{aligned} x &= v \cos \theta . t - \frac{a \sin \beta}{2} . t^2 \\ y &= v \sin \theta . t - \frac{a \cos \beta}{2} . t^2 \end{aligned} \right\} ;$$

velocity in
$$\left. \begin{aligned} x &= v \cos \theta - a \sin \beta . t \\ y &= v \sin \theta - a \cos \beta . t \end{aligned} \right\}$$

Then by question, when $\dot{y} = 0$, the velocity in $x = 0$;

$$\therefore \left. \begin{aligned} v \cos \theta - a \sin \beta . t &= 0 \\ v \sin \theta - \frac{a \cos \beta}{2} . t &= 0 \end{aligned} \right\} ;$$

$$\therefore t = \frac{v \cos \theta}{a \sin \beta} = \frac{2v \sin \theta}{a \cos \beta} .$$

Whence $\cot \theta = 2 \tan \beta$, the condition required.

And for this value of t,

$$x = (a \sin \beta . t) t - \frac{a \sin \beta}{2} . t^2$$

$$= \frac{2v^2 \sin \beta}{a} . \frac{1}{3 \sin^2 \beta + 1} .$$

9. A number of points, moving from the same initial position in the same plane, describe equal parabolas, their motion being

L.   P affected by the same constant acceleration in the same direction: prove that the locus of the vertices of these parabolas will be an equal parabola.

10. Shew that the space passed over in any time by a point, there being a constant acceleration in the direction of motion, is equal to the space which it would describe uniformly in the same time with the mean between its greatest and least velocities during that time.

11. A number of points start from the same position with different velocities, the directions of which are in one plane: there is a constant acceleration in the direction perpendicular to this plane. Shew that the extremities of the latera recta of the parabolas described lie on a cone whose vertical angle $= 2 \tan^{-1} 2$.

12. Two points begin to move with equal velocities in parallel directions: the line joining their initial positions is the direction of a constant acceleration affecting the motion of both. Shew that tangents drawn to the path of the one will cut off from the path of the other arcs described in equal times.

CHAPTER IV.

13. A point is moving in an ellipse, the acceleration being continually towards the focus S. When it arrives at B (the extremity of the minor axis) the acceleration becomes constantly directed to a point S' in SB, the law of its variation being the same, and its magnitude at all equal distances being one-eighth of what it was before; having given $S'B = \frac{1}{5} SB$, shew that the periodic time is unchanged, and find the minor axis of the new orbit.

This is a case of the motion in Art. 76.

In the original orbit, at B,

$$v^2 = \frac{2\lambda}{SB} - \frac{\lambda}{a}.$$

In the new one, $v'^2 = \frac{2\lambda'}{S'B} - \frac{\lambda'}{a'}.$

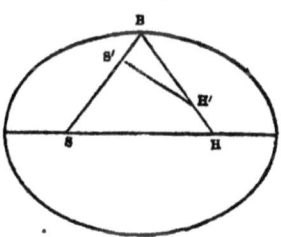

And we have

$$v' = v, \quad S'B = \frac{1}{5} . SB,$$

$$\lambda' = \frac{1}{8}\lambda, \quad SB = a.$$

Whence we obtain $a' = \dfrac{a}{2}$.

And the period $= \dfrac{2\pi a'^{\frac{1}{2}}}{\sqrt{\lambda'}} = \dfrac{2\pi a^{\frac{1}{2}}}{\sqrt{\lambda}}$, the same as in the old orbit.

The other focus of the new orbit evidently lies in BH; let it be H'.

Then $S'B + BH' = 2a' = a$; $S'B = \dfrac{a}{5}$; $\cos \dfrac{1}{2} SBH = \dfrac{b}{a}$;

$S'H'^2$, or $4(a'^2 - b'^2) = S'B^2 + BH'^2 - 2S'B \cdot BH' \cos SBH$,

whence $b' = \dfrac{2}{5} b$.

14. If a point describe an ellipse, the acceleration being towards the center, the locus of the middle points of the chords of all arcs described in equal times, is a similar ellipse.

Let PQ be one of the arcs, and let the ordinate of P, Q meet the auxiliary circle in P', Q'.

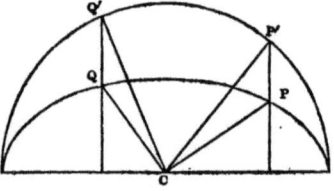

Let ϕ, ψ be the eccentric angles belonging to P, Q.

The sectorial area CPQ

$$= \dfrac{b}{a} \cdot \text{area } CP'Q' = \dfrac{1}{2} ab (\psi - \phi);$$

therefore as the time of describing it is constant, $\psi - \phi$ is constant, $= \epsilon$ say.

The co-ordinates of P, Q are $a \cos \phi$, $b \sin \phi$; $a \cos \psi$, $b \sin \psi$, and those of the middle point of PQ are

$$x = \dfrac{a}{2} (\cos \phi + \cos \psi) = a \cos \left(\phi + \dfrac{\epsilon}{2}\right) \cos \dfrac{\epsilon}{2}$$
$$y = \dfrac{b}{2} (\sin \phi + \sin \psi) = b \sin \left(\phi + \dfrac{\epsilon}{2}\right) \cos \dfrac{\epsilon}{2}$$;

therefore the locus of x, y is an ellipse whose axes are

$$2a \cos \dfrac{\epsilon}{2}, \quad 2b \cos \dfrac{\epsilon}{2}.$$

15. If a point be describing an ellipse, the acceleration being towards the focus; its velocity at any point may be resolved into two constant velocities in directions perpendicular to the radius vector and the major axis, and respectively proportional to the major axis and the distance between the foci.

Let SP, HZ meet in W when produced.

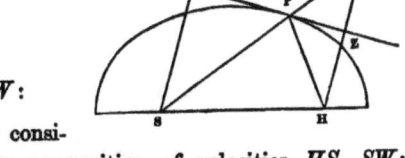

The velocity at $P = \dfrac{h}{SY}$,

and $\therefore \propto HZ$; i.e. $\propto HW$:

and a velocity HW may be considered as resulting from the composition of velocities HS, SW: $SW =$ major axis; and the lines HW, HS, SW are respectively perpendicular to the tangent, and the directions mentioned in the question.

16. A point is moving in an ellipse, the acceleration being towards the center: if the velocity at any point be slightly increased by $\dfrac{1}{n}$th of itself, find the consequent changes in the axes of the ellipse.

If the body be at the extremity of one of the equal conjugate diameters when this takes place, shew that each axis is increased by $\dfrac{1}{2n}$th of itself, and the apse line regredes through a small angle whose circular measure is $\dfrac{1}{n} \cdot \dfrac{ab}{a^2 - b^2}$.

The new orbit will lie as the dotted curve. Using the notation in Arts. 68 and following, and employing suffixed letters for the new orbit, we have

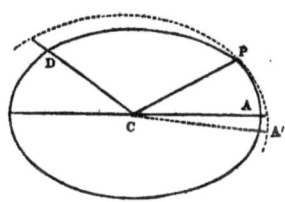

$$\sqrt{\lambda(a^2 + b^2 - r^2)} = v, \qquad \sqrt{\lambda(a_1^2 + b_1^2 - r^2)} = \left(1 + \frac{1}{n}\right)v \dots\dots(1);$$

$$vr\sin\iota = h, \qquad \left(1 + \frac{1}{n}\right)v.r\sin\iota = h_1 \atop ab = \frac{h}{\sqrt{\lambda}}, \qquad a_1 b_1 = \frac{h_1}{\sqrt{\lambda}} \Bigg\};$$

$$\therefore \ a_1 b_1 = \left(1 + \frac{1}{n}\right)ab \dots\dots\dots\dots(2).$$

And if $ACP = \theta$, $A'CP = \theta_1$,

$$\frac{\cos^2\theta}{a^2} + \frac{\sin^2\theta}{b^2} = \frac{1}{r^2} = \frac{\cos^2\theta_1}{a_1^2} + \frac{\sin^2\theta_1}{b_1^2} \dots\dots(3),$$

these equations determine a_1, b_1 and θ_1.

And we must bear in mind that $\frac{1}{n}$ is small, and $\therefore \theta_1 - \theta$, $a_1 - a$, $b_1 - b$ are small.

Second part.

Here we have $\tan\theta = \frac{b}{a}$, whence $r = \sqrt{\frac{a^2 + b^2}{2}}$;

and let $a_1 - a$, $b_1 - b$, $\theta_1 - \theta = a, \beta, \phi$.

Then from (1) we have

$$(a + a)^2 + (b + \beta)^2 - \frac{a^2 + b^2}{2} = \left(1 + \frac{1}{n}\right)^2 . \frac{a^2 + b^2}{2}.$$

From (2) we have

$$(a + a)(b + \beta) = \left(1 + \frac{1}{n}\right)ab.$$

Neglecting squares and products of the small quantities $a, \beta, \frac{1}{n}$, these become

$$aa + b\beta = \frac{1}{2n}(a^2 + b^2) \atop a\beta + ba = \frac{1}{n}ab \Bigg\};$$

whence $a = \frac{a}{2n}$, $\beta = \frac{b}{2n}$.

From (3) we have $\dfrac{2}{a^2+b^2} = \dfrac{\cos^2(\theta+\phi)}{(a+a)^2} + \dfrac{\sin^2(\theta+\phi)}{(b+\beta)^2}$,

and putting $\cos\phi = 1$, $\sin\phi = \phi$, this becomes

$$\frac{2}{a^2+b^2} = \frac{1}{a^2}\left(1-\frac{2a}{a}\right)(\cos^2\theta - 2\phi.\cos\theta\sin\theta)$$

$$+ \frac{1}{b^2}\left(1-\frac{2\beta}{b}\right)(\sin^2\theta + 2\phi.\sin\theta\cos\theta),$$

whence $\phi.\cos\theta\sin\theta\left(\dfrac{1}{b^2}-\dfrac{1}{a^2}\right) = \dfrac{a}{a^2}\cos^2\theta + \dfrac{\beta}{b^2}\sin^2\theta$;

$$\therefore \phi = \frac{1}{n}\cdot\frac{ab}{a^2-b^2}.$$

17. If a point describe a parabola, the acceleration being towards the focus; shew that the time of describing any arc bounded by a focal chord $\propto$ (length of chord)$^{\frac{3}{2}}$.

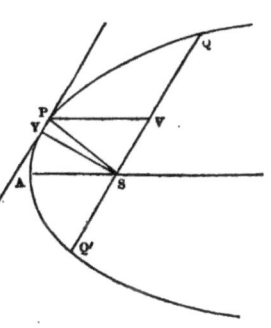

Here $QV^2 = 4SP.PV$,

and $SP = PV$;

$\therefore SP$ or $PV = \dfrac{QV}{2}$.

And area QPQ'

$$= \frac{2}{3}QQ'.PV.\sin PVQ$$

$$= \frac{4}{3}QV.\frac{QV}{2}\cdot\frac{SY}{SP}$$

$$= \frac{4}{3}QV.SY;$$

therefore time of description

$$= \frac{2\text{ area }QPQ'}{h} = \frac{8}{3}\cdot\frac{QV.SY}{h} = \frac{8}{3}\cdot\frac{QV}{\text{velocity at }P}$$

$$= \frac{8}{3}\cdot\frac{QV}{\sqrt{\dfrac{2\lambda}{SP}}}, \text{ which } \propto QV^{\frac{3}{2}}.$$

Δ. This might be solved as in Art. 88.

For we have $\dfrac{c}{r} = 1 + \cos\theta$, $\lambda = \dfrac{h^2}{c}$.

And the time required $= \dfrac{1}{h} \displaystyle\int_{\beta-\pi}^{\beta} r^2 d\theta$, where $ASQ = \beta$,

which $= \dfrac{4}{\sqrt{\lambda}} c^{\frac{3}{2}} (\sin\beta)^{-3}$.

And the chord $QQ' = \dfrac{c}{1 + \cos\beta} + \dfrac{c}{1 + \cos(\beta - \pi)} = \dfrac{2c}{\sin^2\beta}$;

therefore the time ∞ (chord)$^{\frac{3}{2}}$.

Δ. 18. A number of points move in hyperbolas, starting from their vertices at the same instant; the directions of the accelerations pass through the common center, and their magnitudes are equal at all equal distances. Shew that if the major axes coincide, the points will always lie in a common ordinate: and if the asymptotes coincide, they will always lie in a straight line through the center.

From Art. 70, note, we have, for any one of the moving points,

$$x = A\epsilon^{\sqrt{\lambda}.t} + A'\epsilon^{-\sqrt{\lambda}.t} \Big\}$$
$$y = B\epsilon^{\sqrt{\lambda}.t} + B'\epsilon^{-\sqrt{\lambda}.t} \Big\}.$$

Initially $x = a$, $y = 0$, $\dfrac{dx}{dt} = 0$, $\dfrac{dy}{dt} = \sqrt{\lambda}.t$;

$$\therefore x = \dfrac{a}{2}(\epsilon^{\sqrt{\lambda}.t} + \epsilon^{-\sqrt{\lambda}.t}) \Big]$$
$$y = \dfrac{b}{2}(\epsilon^{\sqrt{\lambda}.t} - \epsilon^{-\sqrt{\lambda}.t}) \Big].$$

At any assigned instant of time, let $x_1 y_1$, $x_2 y_2$, &c. be the co-ordinates of the points; $a_1 b_1$, $a_2 b_2$, &c. being the elements of their paths.

Then as λ is the same for all,

If $a_1 = a_2 = $ &c., we shall have $x_1 = x_2 = $ &c.

And if $\dfrac{a_1}{b_1} = \dfrac{a_2}{b_2} = $ &c., $\dfrac{x_1}{y_1} = \dfrac{x_2}{y_2} = $ &c.

Δ. 19. To find the law of acceleration towards the node of a lemniscate, in order that a point may move in that curve.

Here $r^2 = a^2 \cos 2\theta$, or $u = a^{-1}\sqrt{\sec 2\theta}$;

$$\therefore \frac{d^2u}{d\theta^2} = a^{-1}\sqrt{\sec 2\theta}\,(3\sec^2 2\theta - 1)$$

$$= u\,(3a^4u^4 - 1);$$

$$\therefore a = h^2u^2\left(u + \frac{d^2u}{d\theta^2}\right) = 3a^4h^2u^7, \text{ which } \propto (\text{distance})^{-7}.$$

Δ. 20. The acceleration towards a fixed point is $\lambda(r^3 - a^4r)$ at distance r: a point is initially moving with velocity $\sqrt{\tfrac{2}{3}\lambda a^4}$ in a direction at right angles to its initial distance (a) from the fixed point. Find the orbit described.

Here $h = a\sqrt{\tfrac{2}{3}\lambda a^4}$,

$$\frac{d^2u}{d\theta^2} + u = \lambda\,(u^{-3} - a^4u^{-1})\cdot\frac{1}{h^2u^2}$$

$$= \frac{3}{2a^6}\left(\frac{1}{u^7} - \frac{a^4}{u^5}\right);$$

$$\therefore \left(\frac{du}{d\theta}\right)^2 + u^2 = \frac{3}{2a^6}\left(-\frac{1}{3u^6} + \frac{a^4}{u^4}\right) + C.$$

Initially $\dfrac{du}{d\theta} = 0$, $u = \dfrac{1}{a}$; $\therefore C = 0$;

$$\therefore \frac{du}{d\theta} = \frac{3}{2a^6}\left(\frac{a^4}{u^4} - \frac{1}{3u^6}\right) - u^2;$$

$$\therefore \theta - \beta = \sqrt{2}\cdot a^4\int\frac{u^3\,du}{\sqrt{3a^4u^4 - 1 - 2a^6u^8}}$$

$$= \frac{1}{4}\int\frac{d\cdot(au)^4}{\sqrt{\frac{1}{16} - \left(a^4u^4 - \frac{3}{4}\right)^2}} = \frac{1}{4}\sin^{-1}(4a^4u^4 - 3);$$

$$\therefore \frac{4a^4}{r^4} - 3 = \sin 4\,(\theta - \beta).$$

Initially $r = a$, $\theta = 0$; $\therefore$ $1 = -\sin 4\beta$;

whence $\dfrac{4a^4}{r^4} = 3 + \sin\left(4\theta + \dfrac{\pi}{2}\right)$,

or $\dfrac{a^4}{r^4} = \cos^4\theta + \sin^4\theta$;

$\therefore$ $x^4 + y^4 = a^4$; the equation to the path.

Δ. 21. Acceleration $= \lambda r + \dfrac{2\lambda a^3}{r^3}$.* A point is initially moving with a velocity $2a\sqrt{3\lambda}$ at right angles to its initial distance a: shew that it will come to a second apse at distance $3a$.

Here $h = (2a\sqrt{3\lambda})\,a$,

$$\dfrac{d^2u}{d\theta^2} + u = \dfrac{1}{h^2u^2}\left(\dfrac{\lambda}{u} + 2\lambda a^3 u^3\right)$$

$$= \dfrac{1}{12a^4}(u^{-3} + 2a^3);$$

$\therefore$ $\left(\dfrac{du}{d\theta}\right)^2 + u^2 = \dfrac{1}{6a^4}\left(-\dfrac{u^{-2}}{2} + 2a^3 u\right) + C.$

Initially $u = \dfrac{1}{a}$, $\dfrac{du}{d\theta} = 0$; $\therefore$ $C = \dfrac{3}{4a^2}$.

For any other apse $\dfrac{du}{d\theta} = 0$; therefore the apsidal distances are determined by the equation

$$u^2 = \dfrac{1}{6a^4}\left(-\dfrac{u^{-2}}{2} + 2a^3 u\right) + \dfrac{3}{4a^2},$$

or $a^4 u^4 - \dfrac{1}{3}a^3 u^3 - \dfrac{3}{4}a^2 u^2 + \dfrac{1}{12} = 0$,

whence $au = 1$, or $\dfrac{1}{3}$;

the first of which gives the original apsidal distance, the other gives an apsidal distance $3a$.

---

* In such cases as this, the acceleration is supposed to be towards the origin unless the contrary be distinctly expressed.

L.

Q

Δ. 22. The motion of a point is affected by an acceleration in an unvarying direction, whose magnitude varies as the chord of curvature of the path drawn in that direction; shew that the normal acceleration is constant, and determine the path.

Take the given direction to be parallel to the axis of x,

then

$$\frac{d^2s}{dt^2} = \left(\lambda\rho\frac{dy}{ds}\right)\frac{dx}{ds} \Bigg] \; ;$$
$$\frac{v^2}{\rho} = \left(\lambda\rho\frac{dy}{ds}\right)\frac{dy}{ds} \Bigg]$$

$$\therefore v^2 = \lambda\left(\rho\frac{dy}{ds}\right),$$

and $\dfrac{dy}{ds} = \sin\phi$,

and if we choose the axes properly we may have ϕ initially $= \dfrac{\pi}{2}$.

It is evident moreover that ϕ diminishes with an increase of s;

$$\therefore v = -\sqrt{\lambda}\,.\,\rho\sin\phi = -\sqrt{\lambda}\frac{ds}{d\phi}\sin\phi\;;$$

$$\therefore \frac{d\phi}{dt} = -\sqrt{\lambda}\,.\,\sin\phi.$$

Then $\dfrac{ds}{dt} = -\sqrt{\lambda}\,.\,\sin\phi\dfrac{ds}{d\phi}\;;$

$$\therefore \frac{d^2s}{dt^2} = \lambda\sin\phi\left(\sin\phi\frac{d^2s}{d\phi^2} + \cos\phi\frac{ds}{d\phi}\right),$$

and the right-hand member of the first equation is

$$= \sqrt{\lambda}\,.\,v\frac{dx}{ds} = \sqrt{\lambda}\frac{ds}{dt}\cos\phi = -\lambda\sin\phi\cos\phi\frac{ds}{d\phi},$$

whence we have $\dfrac{d^2s}{d\phi^2} = -2\cot\phi\dfrac{ds}{d\phi}\;;$

$$\therefore \frac{ds}{d\phi} = -c\,\mathrm{cosec}^2\phi\;;$$

$$\therefore s = -c\cot\phi\;;$$

the constant being determined by the condition that

$$s = 0, \text{ when } \phi = \frac{\pi}{2}.$$

This shews that the path is a catenary.

The normal acceleration

$$= \lambda\rho \left(\frac{dy}{ds}\right)^2 = -\lambda \frac{ds}{d\phi} \sin^2\phi = \lambda c,$$

which is constant.

23.　If a point be moving in an ellipse, the acceleration being towards the focus, shew that the mean proportional between its velocities at the extremities of any diameter is constant.

24.　If the velocities at any number of points of an ellipse described about the focus be in Arithmetical progression, the velocities at the opposite extremities of the diameters passing through those points will be in Harmonic progression.

25.　Two parabolas have the same axis, and the vertex of one of them lies half way between the focus and vertex of the other, which is intersected by the first at the extremities LL' of its latus rectum. If the accelerations affecting the motions of points that describe these parabolas be towards the respective foci, compare the times of moving from L to L'.

$$\left[\frac{4}{9} \cdot \sqrt{\frac{2\lambda'}{\lambda}} \cdot \right]$$

26.　Acceleration ∞ (distance)$^{-2}$. A point is describing a circle with velocity V in a periodic time P: if a velocity nV be communicated to it in the direction towards the center, shew that a diameter of the circle is the latus rectum of the new orbit, and that the period in the new orbit is $P(1 - n^2)^{-\frac{3}{2}}$.

27.　A point is describing an ellipse, the acceleration being towards the center; when it is at its greatest distance, its velocity is suddenly increased in the ratio of $m : 1$; find the eccentricity of the new orbit, and explain the result when the eccentricity of the original orbit is $< \dfrac{\sqrt{m^2 - 1}}{m}$.

[Eccentricity $= \sqrt{m^2e^2 - (m^2 - 1)}$.

When $e < \dfrac{\sqrt{m^2 - 1}}{m}$, the major-axis of the new orbit is in the direction of the minor-axis of the original one, and its eccentricity $= \sqrt{\dfrac{m^2 - 1 - m^2e^2}{m^2(1 - e^2)}}$].

28. Acceleration $\propto$ (distance)$^{-2}$. A point is initially at a distance of 32 feet, and is moving with a velocity of 100 feet per minute: the velocity necessary for it to describe a circular orbit is 80 feet per minute. Find the periodic time.

[8·68488...minutes.]

29. Acceleration $\propto$ (distance)$^{-2}$. A point describing an ellipse is at one extremity of the minor-axis; shew how the velocity must be changed that the point may proceed to describe a parabola; and shew that the axis of the parabola will pass through the other extremity of the minor-axis.

[The velocity must be increased in the ratio of $\sqrt{2} : 1$.]

30. A point is describing an ellipse, the acceleration being towards the focus: if the magnitude of the acceleration and of the square of the velocity be doubled, what is the effect on the periodic time ?

[It is doubled.]

31. A point is describing a parabola about the focus, and when it arrives at L, the extremity of the latus rectum, its velocity is diminished in the ratio of $\sqrt{2} : 1$; find the position and axes of the new orbit.

[L is the extremity of the minor-axis, which is normal to the parabola.]

32. A point is describing a parabola about the focus S, and when it arrives at a given point Q in its path, the direction of the acceleration is suddenly reversed so as to be always away from S: determine the nature, position, and dimensions of the new orbit.

[It is an hyperbola, S being the exterior focus: the other focus lies in the diameter of the parabola at Q, and its distance from $Q = \frac{1}{2} . SQ$.]

Δ. 33. A point moving from the origin in the direction of the axis of y with a velocity c describes a parabola $y^2 = 4ax$, its motion being effected by an acceleration $-\lambda y$ in the direction of y, and by another in the direction of x; shew that its velocity at any point $= \sqrt{\lambda \left(1 + \dfrac{y^2}{4a^2}\right)(c^2 - y^2)}$.

Δ. 34. A curve $y = f(x)$, (which touches the axis of y at the origin) is described by a point, there being a constant acceleration a in the direction of x, and another in the direction of y: shew that this acceleration

$$= 2a \sqrt{x} \cdot \frac{d}{dx}\left(\sqrt{x}\,\frac{dy}{dx}\right).$$

Δ. 35. If the motion of a point be affected by two equal accelerations λy in directions of x and y, find the path.

$$\left[y = A\epsilon^{\frac{\sqrt{\lambda}}{c}(x - c - y)} + B\epsilon^{-\frac{\sqrt{\lambda}}{c}(x - c - y)}.\right]$$

Δ. 36. The acceleration affecting the motion of a point P varies as the distance from a point Q, which moves uniformly in the circumference of a circle, being constantly directed from Q: shew that when the point Q arrives successively at any given position on the circle, the point P will be always situated on a certain hyperbola.

Δ. 37. The acceleration towards a fixed point, at distance $r = \dfrac{3\lambda}{r^3} + \dfrac{2\lambda a^2}{r^5}$. A point is initially moving in a direction making an angle $\tan^{-1}\frac{1}{2}$ with the initial distance a, and with a velocity equal to that with which, affected by the above acceleration, it would describe a circle of radius a: determine its path.

$$\left[r = a \cot\left(\theta + \frac{\pi}{4}\right).\right]$$

Δ. 38. Acceleration $= \lambda\left(\dfrac{8a^2}{r^5} - \dfrac{3}{r^3}\right)$. A point is initially at an apse at distance a, the space due to its initial velocity being $\dfrac{a}{10}$: determine the path.

$$[r = a \cos 2\theta.]$$

Δ. 39. Acceleration $\propto$ (distance)$^{-2}$. A point is initially moving in a direction inclined at an angle of $45°$ to its distance (a) with a velocity $=\dfrac{2}{\sqrt{3}} \times$ that which it would acquire in moving from an infinite distance to its initial distance, starting from rest, if affected by the above acceleration. Find the orbit described.

$$\left[\frac{2a}{r} = (\sqrt{2}+1)\epsilon^{\frac{1}{\sqrt{2}}\theta} - (\sqrt{2}-1)\epsilon^{-\frac{1}{\sqrt{2}}\theta}.\right]$$

CHAPTERS VI. VII.

40. If the unit of force be that which will just support a weight of 5 lbs., and the unit of acceleration be that which, if referred to 1 foot and 1 second as units, is 3 : find the unit of mass.

The unit of acceleration is that of 1 yard per second.

The unit of mass is that on which the unit of force (5 lbs.) produces the unit of acceleration (1 yard per second) ; see Art. 107 ;

therefore the unit of mass is that on which the force of 1 lb. would produce the acceleration of $\dfrac{1}{5}$ yard per second.

But on the mass weighing 1 lb., the force of 1 lb. produces an acceleration g, or 32·2 feet per second;

therefore on the mass weighing 32·2 lbs., the force of 1 lb. produces an acceleration of 1 foot per second;

therefore on the mass weighing $\dfrac{5}{3}$ of 32·2 lbs., the force of 1 lb. produces an acceleration of $\dfrac{3}{5}$ ft., or $\dfrac{1}{5}$ yd. per second;

therefore the unit of mass is that quantity of matter, the weight of which is $\dfrac{5}{3}$ (32·2) lbs., or 53⅔ lbs.

41. The period of the moon round the earth is 27⅓ days, nearly: her mean distance from the earth's center is nearly $= 60 \times$ earth's radius. Calculate approximately the value of the acceleration of gravity at the earth's surface.

The earth's attraction ∞ (distance)$^{-2}$;

therefore the motion is that in Art. 76, and the period $= \dfrac{2\pi}{\sqrt{\lambda}} a^{\frac{3}{2}}$. (Art. 84, or Newton, § iij., Prop. 15).

Let the earth's radius be the unit of space, and 1 day the unit of time: then $a = 60$; $\lambda =$ acceleration produced by the earth's attraction on a body placed at the unit of distance from its center, i.e. on a body at the earth's surface, and therefore λ measures the acceleration of gravity.

And we have $27\frac{1}{3} = \dfrac{2\pi}{\sqrt{\lambda}} 60^{\frac{3}{2}}$.

Whence $\lambda = \dfrac{10 \cdot 9 \cdot 60^3}{41^2}$, putting $\pi = \sqrt{10}$.

If we wish this to be expressed in terms of feet and seconds, we must transform it after the manner of Art. 27, and putting the earth's radius $= 4000$ miles nearly, we have

$$\lambda = \left(\frac{10 \cdot 9 \cdot 60^3}{41^2}\right) \cdot \frac{4000 \cdot 1760 \cdot 3}{(24 \cdot 60 \cdot 60)^2} = 32 \cdot 7 \dots$$

42. If a body be shot up vertically at a place in latitude l, it will describe a curve of which the equation is

$$2\omega^2 \cos^2 l \cdot y^2 - 2V\omega \cos l \cdot xy + gx^2 = 0,$$

where x, y are the horizontal and vertical co-ordinates from the point of projection, ω the earth's angular velocity, V the velocity of projection; and all variation of gravity in magnitude and direction is neglected.

The linear velocity of the point A on the earth's surface is $\omega r \cos l$, r being the earth's radius;

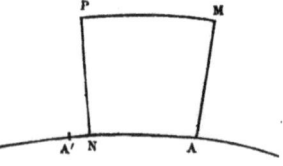

therefore the body has initially a horizontal velocity $\omega r \cos l$, and a vertical velocity V;

therefore if P be its position in space at time t, A its initial position, AM vertical, PM horizontal,

$$AM = Vt - \frac{gt^2}{2}; \quad PM = \omega r \cos l \cdot t.$$

Draw PN towards the earth's center; then if the point of projection A be transferred to A' at the instant under consideration,

$$AA' = \omega r \cos l . t, \quad A'N = x, \quad NP = y;$$

$$\therefore \; x = AA' - \frac{r}{r+y} .. PM = \frac{y}{r+y} \, \omega r \cos l . t,$$

and $y = Vt - \dfrac{gt^2}{2} = Vx \dfrac{r+y}{y} . \dfrac{1}{\omega r \cos l} - \dfrac{gx^2}{2} \left(\dfrac{r+y}{y} \right)^2 . \dfrac{1}{\omega^2 r^2 \cos^2 l}$,

and putting $\dfrac{r+y}{r} = 1$, this becomes

$$2\omega^2 \cos^2 l . y^2 - 2V\omega \cos l . xy + gx^2 = 0.$$

43. In what time will a force which will just support 5 lbs. weight, move a mass of 10 lbs. weight through 50 feet on a horizontal plane, and what will be the velocity at the end of that time?

$\left[2\frac{1}{2} \text{ sec.} ; \; 40 \text{ feet per sec.} ; \text{ if we consider } g = 32 \text{ feet per sec.} \right]$

44. Of all comets moving in the ecliptic in parabolic orbits, that which has the latus rectum of its orbit equal to the diameter of the earth's orbit, considered circular, will remain within the latter for the longest period.

45. From a given point particles are projected in all directions so as to describe parabolas about a center of force, the attraction to which $\propto (\text{distance})^{-2}$. Find the locus of the vertices.

$$\left[r = c \cos \frac{\theta}{2} . \right]$$

CHAPTER VIII.

46. A pendulum is found to make 640 vibrations at the equator in the same time as that in which it makes 641 at Greenwich: if a string will just sustain 80 lbs. at Greenwich, how many such lbs. will it sustain at the equator?

Let g be the acceleration of gravity at Greenwich, and g' that at the equator; M, M' the quantities of matter which the string will sustain at Greenwich and the equator respectively.

Then Mg, $M'g'$ are the forces exerted in these cases by the string (Art. 107);

$$\therefore Mg = M'g' = 80 \text{ lbs.}$$

Also $640 \cdot \pi \sqrt{\dfrac{l}{g}} = 641 \cdot \pi \sqrt{\dfrac{\dot{l}}{g}}$ (Art. 143);

whence $\dfrac{M'}{M} = \dfrac{g}{g'} = \left(\dfrac{641}{640}\right)^2$;

$$\therefore M'g = \left(\dfrac{641}{640}\right)^2 80 \text{ lbs.} = 80 \frac{1281}{5120} \text{ lbs.}$$

Δ. 47. A particle starts from rest at the top of a sphere of radius a, acted on by its weight and an attractive force varying as the distance towards the lowest point of the sphere : find the pressure on the sphere; and if at the distance a the force produces an acceleration equal to g, when will the particle leave the sphere ?

The motion is evidently in a vertical plane: let this be the plane of the paper, and let P be the position of the particle at time t, AB a vertical diameter,

$$AOP = \theta,$$

λ the acceleration at distance unity towards B.

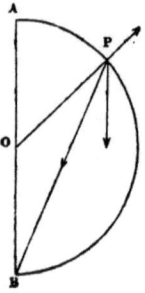

Then $a \dfrac{d^2\theta}{dt^2} = g \sin\theta + \lambda \cdot PB \sin OPB$

$$= (g + \lambda a) \sin\theta,$$

$$a \left(\frac{d\theta}{dt}\right)^2 = g\cos\theta + \lambda \cdot PB \cos OPB - \xi$$

$$= (g + \lambda a)\cos\theta + \lambda a - \xi.$$

From the first, $\left(\dfrac{d\theta}{dt}\right)^2 = 2\dfrac{g + \lambda a}{a}(1 - \cos\theta)$;

$$\therefore \xi = \lambda a + (g + \lambda a)(3\cos\theta - 2).$$

This multiplied by the measure of the mass of the particle gives the pressure on the sphere.

L.   R

The particle leaves the sphere when $\dot{\xi} = 0$,

$$\text{i. e. when } 3 \cos \theta = 2 - \frac{\lambda a}{g + \lambda a}.$$

Also we have $\lambda a = g$; $\therefore \overset{\bullet}{\cos} \theta = \frac{1}{2}$.

Δ. 48. Two equal weights (W) are connected by an extensible string whose natural length is a, and are placed, the one on an inclined plane of angle ι, and the other hanging vertically over the top. If the system be left to itself, shew that at the time t the tension of the string is $2W \cos^2 \left(\frac{\pi}{4} - \frac{\iota}{2} \right) \sin^2 \left(\sqrt{\frac{g}{2a}} \cdot t \right)$; the string being such that either of the weights suspended at one end would stretch it to a length $2a$, it being initially stretched without tension in a vertical plane.

Here $W = E$; and if ξ be the acceleration due to the tension at time t, the length of the string $= a \left(1 + \frac{T}{E} \right) = a \left(1 + \frac{\xi}{g} \right)$.

Let c be the length initially on the plane,

s the length on the plane at time t;

then the distance of the hanging particle from the top of the plane is

$$a \left(1 + \frac{\xi}{g} \right) - s, \quad = x \text{ say.}$$

$$\text{Wherefore } \frac{d^2 x}{dt^2} = g - \xi;$$

and for the motion of the other $\dfrac{d^2 s}{dt^2} = g \sin \iota - \xi$.

$$\therefore g (1 + \sin \iota) - 2 \xi = \overline{\frac{d}{dt}}\Big|^2 (x + s) = \frac{a}{g} \frac{d^2 \xi}{dt^2},$$

$$\text{or } \frac{d^2 \xi}{dt^2} + \frac{2g}{a} \xi = \frac{g^2}{a} (1 + \sin \iota);$$

$$\therefore \xi = \frac{g^2}{a} (1 + \sin \iota) \div \frac{2g}{a} + A \cos \left(\sqrt{\frac{2g}{a}} t - \beta \right).$$

Initially $x = a - c$, $s = c$, $\dfrac{dx}{dt} = 0$, $\dfrac{ds}{dt} = 0$;

$$\therefore \xi = 0, \quad \dfrac{d\xi}{dt} = 0;$$

$$\therefore \xi = \dfrac{g}{2}(1 + \sin \iota) - \dfrac{g}{2}(1 + \sin \iota) \cos\left(\sqrt{\dfrac{2g}{a}} \cdot t\right);$$

$$\therefore T = 2W \cos^2\left(\dfrac{\pi}{4} - \dfrac{\iota}{2}\right) \sin^2\left(\sqrt{\dfrac{g}{2a}} \cdot t\right).$$

Δ. 49. A straight tube of length l revolves with an angular velocity $\sqrt{\dfrac{g}{l}}$ about a vertical axis through its lowest point, being inclined to it at the angle $\dfrac{\pi}{3}$. Shew that if a particle be placed in the tube just above its position of relative equilibrium, the latus rectum of the parabola described after leaving the tube $= \dfrac{13}{8}l$.

Let OP be the tube, OR the vertical axis,

$ON = z$, $NP = r$, which together with θ (the angle through which NP has revolved in a horizontal plane) determine the position of P;

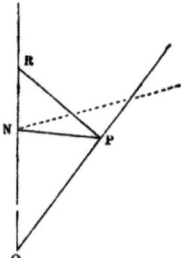

$\xi =$ the acceleration in PR, $\zeta =$ that perpendicular to PR and PO, due to the constraint.

Then
$$\left.\begin{array}{c} \dfrac{d^2r}{dt^2} - r\left(\dfrac{d\theta}{dt}\right)^2 = -\xi \cos \dfrac{\pi}{3} \\[2mm] \dfrac{1}{r}\dfrac{d}{dt}\left(r^2 \dfrac{d\theta}{dt}\right) = \zeta \\[2mm] \dfrac{d^2z}{dt^2} = \xi \sin \dfrac{\pi}{3} - g \end{array}\right\}.$$

Also if $OP = s$, $r = s \sin \dfrac{\pi}{3}$, $z = s \cos \dfrac{\pi}{3}$, $\theta = \sqrt{\dfrac{g}{l}} \cdot t$,

whence $\dfrac{d^2s}{dt^2} - \dfrac{3g}{4l}s = -\dfrac{g}{2}$.

For relative equilibrium s is constant, and $\therefore = \dfrac{2l}{3}$.

For the motion $\left(\dfrac{ds}{dt}\right)^2 - \dfrac{3g}{4l} s^2 = - gs + C.$

Initially $\dfrac{ds}{dt} = 0, \quad s = \dfrac{2l}{3};$

and at the end of the constrained motion $s = l;$

therefore at this instant $\dfrac{ds}{dt} = \sqrt{\dfrac{1}{12} gl};$

this is in the direction OP.

The horizontal and vertical components of this velocity will be

$$\sqrt{\dfrac{1}{16} gl}, \quad \sqrt{\dfrac{1}{48} gl}.$$

There is also a velocity perpendicular to PR and PO, which

$= r \dfrac{d\theta}{dt},$

and therefore $= \sqrt{\dfrac{3}{4} gl}$ at the end of the constrained motion:
this is horizontal;

therefore the whole horizontal velocity

$$= \sqrt{\dfrac{1}{16} gl + \dfrac{3}{4} gl} = \sqrt{\dfrac{13}{16} gl},$$

therefore the latus rectum of the parabola described $= \dfrac{13}{8} l.$
(Art. 45.)

50. How must the earth's angular velocity be changed that a body may just lose its weight at the equator?

$$\left[\text{To} \ \dfrac{9}{2} \sqrt{\dfrac{32 \cdot 2}{33}} \ \text{(circular measure) per hour.} \right]$$

51. A right-angled triangle has its hypotenuse vertical: if three particles slide from rest down the three sides, the velocities acquired will be proportional to the sides.

52. Two bodies are dropped from points P, Q on to a smooth inclined plane, and reach the bottom of it with the same velocity: prove that the line PQ is perpendicular to the plane.

53. A double hollow cone is formed by the revolution of a right-angled triangle about its hypotenuse which is vertical. If any number of particles be let fall at the same instant from different points in the interior surface of the upper cone, and run down the surface of the lower, they will all arrive simultaneously at its vertex.

54. A heavy body is projected up a rough plane of inclination 60°, with the velocity due to falling freely through 12 feet, and just reaches the top of the plane: given that the body will rest on the plane if it be inclined at any angle not exceeding 30°, find its altitude.

[9 feet.]

55. In Atwood's machine, if at the end of each second from the beginning of the motion W be increased, and W' diminished by $\dfrac{1}{n}$ th of their original difference, then at the end of $(n + 1)$ seconds, the system will be at rest.

56. A string charged with $n + m + 1$ equal weights at equal intervals a, which would rest on an inclined plane with m weights hanging over the top, is placed on the plane, passing over a smooth pulley at the top, with the $(m + 1)^{th}$ weight just over: shew that the velocity when the last weight leaves the plane $= \sqrt{nag}$.

57. A string loaded with n equal particles at equal distances a, is placed at rest on a smooth horizontal table with one particle just over the edge, where there is a pulley over which the string passes: find the velocity when the last particle leaves the table.

$$[\sqrt{(n - 1) ga}.]$$

Hence shew that if a heavy string of length c be so placed, its velocity on falling off $= \sqrt{gc}$.

58. A seconds pendulum was too long on a certain day by a quantity a, it was then over-corrected so as to be too short by a during the next day. Shew that the number of minutes gained in the two days $= 1080 \dfrac{a^2}{l^2}$ nearly, when $l =$ the proper length of the pendulum.

59. A seconds pendulum hanging against the smooth face of a slightly inclined wall and swinging in its plane, is observed to lose s seconds in t hours: find the inclination of the wall to the horizon.

$$\left[\sin^{-1}\left(1 - \frac{s}{1800t}\right) \text{ nearly.}\right]$$

60. A smooth tube is bent into the form of a circular arc greater than a semicircle, and placed in a vertical plane with the open ends upwards and in the same horizontal line. Find the velocity with which a ball that exactly fits the tube must be projected from the lowest point so as to pass out at one end and re-enter at the other.

$$\left[\sqrt{ga\,(\sec a + 2 + 2\cos a)}, \text{ the length of the tube being } 2a\,(\pi - a).\right]$$

61. A rigid framework consists of a square base $ABCD$, two uprights EF, GH, rising from E, G, the middle points of AB, CD, and a cross beam FH, the uprights being of such height that AFB, CHD are equilateral triangles: the framework rests on a rough horizontal table, and from FH a heavy body is suspended by a fine string, and oscillates through a semicircle in a vertical plane perpendicular to FH. Prove that the framework will be tilted if its weight do not exceed $\frac{3}{2} \times$ weight of the suspended body.

Δ. 62. An elastic string has its length increased by h when a weight W is suspended from it at rest, and the greatest weight which it can bear is $(n+1)W$: if W be let fall from any height not exceeding $\frac{1}{2}(n^2 + 1)h$ above its position of equilibrium, the string will not be broken.

Δ. 63. A center of attractive force revolves in a horizontal circle of radius a, with the velocity due to falling from the center to the circumference under the action of gravity; its intensity varies as the distance and at a distance a produces an acceleration g. A smooth ring slides on a concentric horizontal circle of radius $2a$, being initially at rest and at its least distance from the center of force; if at time t the distance of the ring from the center of force subtends an angle ϕ at the center of the circles, shew that

$$\tan\frac{\phi}{4} = \frac{\epsilon^{\sqrt{\frac{g}{2a}}\cdot t} - 1}{\epsilon^{\sqrt{\frac{g}{2a}}\cdot t} + 1}.$$

Δ. 64. A smooth circular wire is made to revolve with an uniform angular velocity about a vertical diameter: determine the motion of a small heavy ring placed on it at a given point and initially at rest. Find also the strain on the wire, and the condition that the ring may oscillate.

[For oscillation ω^2 must be $< \dfrac{g}{a} \sec^2 \dfrac{a}{2}$, aa being the initial distance of the ring from the lowest point.]

Δ. 65. A particle moves from rest along the spiral tube $r = \epsilon^{\theta \cot a}$ subject to an attractive force $\propto (\text{distance})^{-2}$ in the pole. If a be its initial distance, find at what time it will reach the pole.

$$\left[\frac{\pi}{\cos a} \sqrt{\frac{a^3}{8\lambda}} \cdot \right]$$

CHAPTER IX.

66. An elastic ball rebounds continually between two parallel vertical planes: shew that the latera recta of the successive parabolic paths decrease in Geometrical progression.

At every impact the vertical velocity is not changed, and the horizontal velocity is reversed in direction and diminished in the ratio of $e : 1$.

Also during the parabolic motion the horizontal velocity is constant.

And by Art. 45 the latus rectum $= \dfrac{2}{g} (\text{horizontal velocity})^2$;

therefore the latera recta form a decreasing Geometrical progression whose common ratio is e^2.

67. Two equal elastic balls are projected with equal velocities from opposite angles of a square lying in a horizontal plane along two of its adjacent sides, and impinge: determine the directions of their subsequent motions.

Let the balls start from A, A': and let xOx' be the diagonal of the square.

It is clear that the impulse will be perpendicular to Ox.

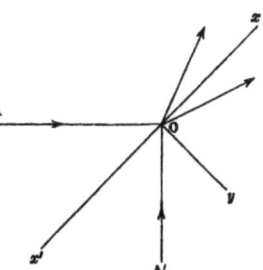

Let v be the velocity of projection of each ball.

Then before impact the velocity of the ball M (which has passed along AO) resolved in the direction Ox is $\dfrac{v}{\sqrt{2}}$,

and its velocity in $Oy = +\dfrac{v}{\sqrt{2}}$.

The velocity of the other ball M' in $Ox = \dfrac{v}{\sqrt{2}}$,

and its velocity in $Oy = -\dfrac{v}{\sqrt{2}}$.

The velocity of each ball in Ox is not affected by the impact, and their velocities in Oy are determined as in Art. 157. We have then in those formulæ to write

$$\frac{v}{\sqrt{2}}, \quad -\frac{v}{\sqrt{2}} \text{ for } V, \ V',$$

and we have also $M' = M$;

therefore after impact the velocity of M in $Oy = -e \cdot \dfrac{v}{\sqrt{2}}$,

and that of M' in $Oy = +e \cdot \dfrac{v}{\sqrt{2}}$,

and their velocities in Ox are both $= \dfrac{v}{\sqrt{2}}$;

therefore they move in directions equally inclined to Ox and on opposite sides of it, with equal velocities $\left(\sqrt{\dfrac{1+e^2}{2}} . v \right)$, and the inclination of the direction of motion of either of them to Ox is $\tan^{-1} e$.

68. A particle is projected from a point, and by rebounding against a horizontal plane describes a series of parabolas. Shew that the vertices and also the foci lie on parabolas.

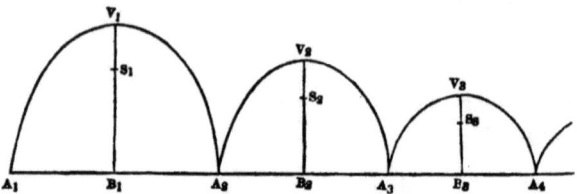

Let u, v be the vertical and horizontal components of the velocity of projection, and let the figure represent the successive parabolic paths.

Then in all these parabolas the horizontal velocity is v.

At the points A_1, A_2, A_3, &c. the vertical velocity

$$= u, \; eu, \; e^2 u, \; \&c.$$

And by Arts. 43, 44, we have

$$\left.\begin{aligned} A_1 B_1 &= \frac{uv}{g} \\ A_2 B_2 &= \frac{euv}{g} \\ A_3 B_3 &= \frac{e^2 uv}{g} \\ \&c. \end{aligned}\right\}, \qquad \left.\begin{aligned} S_1 B_1 &= \frac{u^2 - v^2}{2g} \\ S_2 B_2 &= \frac{e^2 u^2 - v^2}{2g} \\ S_3 B_3 &= \frac{e^4 u^2 - v^2}{2g} \\ \&c. \end{aligned}\right\}, \qquad \left.\begin{aligned} B_1 V_1 &= \frac{u^2}{2g} \\ B_2 V_2 &= \frac{e^2 u^2}{2g} \\ B_3 V_3 &= \frac{e^4 u^2}{2g} \\ \&c. \end{aligned}\right\};$$

$$\therefore \; A_1 B_1 = \frac{uv}{g},$$

$$A_1 B_2 = \frac{uv}{g} (2 + e),$$

$$A_1 B_3 = \frac{uv}{g} \cdot \{ 2 \cdot (1 + e) + e^2 \},$$

$$A_1 B_4 = \frac{uv}{g} \{ 2 (1 + e + e^2) + e^3 \},$$

$$\&c.,$$

these are the horizontal co-ordinates of both foci and vertices, measured from A_1.

L.

8

For the vertices we have (taking the nth of them)

$$x = \frac{uv}{g}\left(2 \cdot \frac{1-e^n}{1-e} + e^n\right), \quad y = \frac{e^{2n-2} \cdot u^2}{2g},$$

whence $e^{2n} = e^2 \cdot \frac{2gy}{u^2};$

$$\therefore x = \frac{uv}{g}\left\{\frac{2}{1-e}\left(1 - e\frac{\sqrt{2gy}}{u}\right) + e \cdot \frac{\sqrt{2gy}}{u}\right\},$$

which is a parabola whose latus rectum

$$= \left(\frac{1+e}{1-e}\right)^2 \cdot \frac{2e^2 v^2}{g}.$$

For the foci,

$$x = \frac{uv}{g}\left\{2 \cdot \frac{1-e^n}{1-e} + e^n\right\}, \quad y = \frac{e^{2n-2}u^2 - v^2}{2g}.$$

Whence $\frac{gx}{uv} = \frac{2}{1-e}(1 - \frac{e}{u}\sqrt{v^2 + 2gy}) + \frac{e}{u}\sqrt{v^2 + 2gy},$

which is a parabola equal to the former.

69. A perfectly elastic particle is moving in a circle, under the action of a force to the center varying as $(\text{distance})^{-2}$, and impinges on a plane perpendicular to the plane of motion and making an angle of 60° with the radius from the point of impact. Find the new orbit, and the time during which the particle is within its former orbit.

Let S be the center of the circle, and the focus of the subsequent orbit.

Q the point of impact, $SQD = 60°$, QT the direction of motion after impact: then as the elasticity is perfect $TQD = 30° = SQT$ (Art. 164).

The (velocity)^2 in the circle $= \frac{\lambda}{a}$.

The (velocity)^2 at Q in the subsequent orbit $= \frac{2\lambda}{SQ} - \frac{\lambda}{a}$.

These are equal; $\therefore a' = a$.

The orbit is therefore an ellipse, and Q is the extremity of the minor-axis.

Draw SC parallel to QT, and QC perpendicular to SC;

therefore C is the center,

and $QC = b' = SQ \sin CSQ = \dfrac{a}{2}$;

therefore the latus rectum $= \dfrac{a}{2}$, and $e' = \dfrac{\sqrt{3}}{2}$.

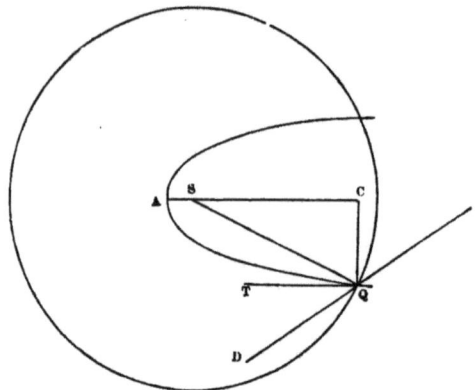

It is manifest that the ellipse will cut the circle again at the other extremity of its minor-axis.

And the time required in the question $= \dfrac{4 \cdot \text{area } ASQ}{h}$

$$= \frac{4 \cdot (ACQ - SCQ)}{h} = \frac{\pi a'b' - 2a'e' \cdot b'}{\sqrt{\dfrac{\lambda a}{4}}} = (\pi - \sqrt{3}) \sqrt{\frac{a^3}{\lambda}}.$$

70. Two bodies fall freely from rest through equal spaces, and impinge on two inclined planes; the ranges on the planes of their parabolic paths after impact are equal; find a relation between their elasticities.

$$[e(1 + e^2) \sin \iota = e'(1 + e'^2) \sin \iota'.]$$

71. A body Q is placed at rest at a given point of a vertical circle, and at the lowest point impinges on a body P at rest, which then runs up an observed arc: determine the elasticity.

[If the arcs over which Q and P pass, subtend angles 2α and

2β at the center, $e = \dfrac{P+Q}{Q} \dfrac{\sin \beta}{\sin \alpha} - 1.]$

72. With what velocity must a ball of given elasticity be projected from a given point in a given direction towards a vertical wall, in order that after striking the wall it may return to the point of projection?

$$\left[\sqrt{ga\left(1+\frac{1}{e}\right)}\operatorname{cosec}2\iota.\right]$$

73. Find the velocity with which a perfectly elastic ball must be projected in a given direction from a point in the side AB of a square $ABCD$, so that after striking each of the other sides it may return to the point of projection, BC being vertical.

$$\left[\sec\iota\sqrt{\frac{ga}{2\left(\tan\iota-1\right)}}\,.\right]$$

74. Two equal and perfectly elastic balls are projected in the same vertical plane from two points in the same horizontal line at a distance $g\dfrac{\sqrt{3}}{2}$ from each other: the former vertically with a velocity g, and the latter at an elevation of $30°$ with a velocity $2g$: determine the motion of each after impact.

[They interchange paths.]

75. Two particles whose common elasticity is $\frac{1}{4}$ are let fall in opposite directions at the same instant from the highest point of a smooth circular tube in a vertical plane: find the ratio of their masses in order that the heavier may remain at rest after the impact, and determine the height to which the other will rise.

[$3:2$; $\frac{1}{2}$. radius.]

76. ABC is a triangle, and $\tan A \tan C = (\tan B)^{2}$; a particle is projected in a direction parallel to CB, and strikes AB, BC successively. Shew that if after the first impact it moves parallel to AC, then after the second it will move parallel to BA.

Also shew that $e^{\frac{1}{2}} + e^{-\frac{1}{2}} = \sec B$.

77. An elastic particle impinges on a rough plane, the impulsive friction being proportional to the impulsive pressure: determine the subsequent motion.

$$\left[\tan\phi = -\frac{1}{e}\left\{\tan\theta - (1+e)\,.\,\mu\right\}.\right]$$